D0328862

MUZZLELOADER HUNTING

©1990 by National Rifle Association of America

All rights reserved. Printed in the United States of America. No part of this book may be reproduced in whole or part without written permission.

Produced by the NRA Hunter Services Division. For information on the Hunter Skills Series, NRA Hunter Clinic Program, or becoming a volunteer hunter clinic instructor, contact the National Rifle Association of America, Hunter Services Division, 1600 Rhode Island Avenue NW, Washington, D.C. 20036-3268. Telephone (202) 828-6240.

Library of Congress Catalog Card Number;
90-83401

Main entry under title:
Muzzleloader Hunting–NRA Hunter Skills Series

ISBN 0-935998-68-3

HS5N5145 (paper back)   HS5N5172 (hard bound)

ACKNOWLEDGEMENTS

Authors

Mike Strandlund, Program Specialist,
   Editorial Productions, NRA Hunter Services Division
Jeff Murray, Field Representative,
   National Muzzle Loading Rifle Association
Doug Pifer, Resource Specialist,
   Editorial Productions, NRA Hunter Services Division

Editor

Mike Strandlund, Program Specialist,
   Editorial Productions, NRA Hunter Services Division

Production Manager

Earl W. Hower, Program Manager, NRA Hunter Skills
   Department

Illustrator

Doug Pifer, Resource Specialist, Editorial Productions,
   NRA Hunter Services Division

Co-Authors and Review Committee

Dr. James W. Carlson, Member NRA Board of Directors,
   Chairman NRA Black Powder Committee,
   Member National Muzzle Loading Rifle Association
   Board of Directors
Alfred W. Hill, Member NRA Black Powder Committee,
   Past Member NRA Board of Directors, Past President
   National Muzzle Loading Rifle Association
Gary Anderson, Executive Director,
   NRA General Operations
Jim Norine, Director, NRA Hunter Services Division
Dennis Eggers, Assistant Director,
   NRA Hunter Services Division
Barry Winner, Program Manager,
   NRA Hunter Education Support Services Department
Kitty Beuchert, Program Manager,
   NRA Hunter Information Department

Robert L. Davis, Jr., Program Manager,
 NRA Youth Hunting Skills Department
Frank Higginson, Manager, Black Powder Department,
 NRA Competitions Division
Dave Messics, Program Specialist,
 NRA Hunter Skills Department
Maxine Moss, Editor Emeritus, *Muzzle Blasts*,
 National Muzzle Loading Rifle Association
Jim Smith, Shooting Sports Program Coordinator,
 Thompson/Center Arms Co., Inc.
Sharon Cunningham, Editor, *Muzzle Blasts*,
 National Muzzle Loading Rifle Association
Bob Staton, Hunter Skills Projects Coordinator,
 Missouri Department of Conservation

The National Rifle Association of America is grateful for the contributions made by the preceding persons, by the National Muzzle Loading Rifle Association, and the government agencies and organizations credited throughout this book.

Photo Credits

Cover Photos by **Mike Strandlund**

Caution: Procedures and techniques outlined in this publication may require special abilities, technical knowledge, or safety considerations. The National Rifle Association of America, its agents, officers, and employees accept no responsibility for the results obtained by persons using these procedures and techniques and disclaim all liability for any consequential injuries or damages.

Mention of products or technical data does not necessarily mean they have been tested by the authors or NRA staff, and does not constitute endorsement or verification by the NRA.

Local restrictions may apply to some techniques, procedures, and products in your area. Check local laws and game regulations before proceeding.

NRA Hunter's Code of Ethics

I will consider myself an invited guest of the landowner, seeking his permission, and conduct myself so that I may be welcome in the future.

I will obey the rules of safe gun handling and will courteously but firmly insist that others who hunt with me do the same.

I will obey all game laws and regulations, and will insist that my companions do likewise.

I will do my best to acquire marksmanship and hunting skills that assure clean, sportsmanlike kills.

I will support conservation efforts that assure good hunting for future generations of Americans.

I will pass along to younger hunters the attitudes and skills essential to a true outdoor sportsman.

NRA Gun Safety Rules

The fundamental NRA rules for safe gun handling are:

- Always keep the gun pointed in a safe direction.
- Always keep your finger off the trigger until ready to shoot.
- Always keep the gun unloaded until ready to use.

When using or storing a gun always follow these NRA rules:

- Be sure the gun is safe to operate.
- Know how to safely use the gun.
- Use only the correct ammunition for your gun.
- Know your target and what is beyond.
- Wear eye and ear protection as appropriate.
- Never use alcohol or drugs before or while shooting.
- Store guns so they are not accessible to unauthorized persons.

Be aware that certain types of guns and many shooting activities require additional safety precautions.

To learn more about gun safety, enroll in an NRA hunter clinic or state hunter education class, or an NRA safety training or basic marksmanship course.

TODAY'S AMERICAN HUNTER

I f you're a hunter, you're one of 20 million Americans who love the outdoors, have a close tie with traditions, and help conserve our natural resources. You know the thrill and beauty of a duck blind at dawn, a whitetail buck sneaking past your stand, a hot-headed, bugling bull elk. With your friends and forefathers you share the rich traditions of knowing wild places and good hunting dogs. Your woodsmanship and appreciation of nature provide food for body and soul.

And through contributions to hunting licenses and stamps, conservation tax funds, and sportsman clubs, you are partly responsible for the dramatic recovery of wildlife and its habitat. Hunters can take great pride—and satisfaction that only hunters know—in the great increases of deer, turkeys, elk, some waterfowl, and other species over the last century.

Your involvement with the National Rifle Association of America is also important to promote conservation and sportsmanship. In NRA, concerned hunters and shooters work together for laws and programs of benefit to the shooting sports. Most important is the education of sportsmen through programs like the nationwide Hunter Clinic Program operated by the NRA Hunter Services Division. Through the program and the Hunter Skills Series of how-to hunting books, America's already admirable hunters can keep improving their skills, safety, responsibility, and sportsmanship to help ensure our country's rich hunting traditions flourish forever.

CONTENTS

Page

Photo by Gerald Almy

WELCOME TO MUZZLELOADER HUNTING

The purpose of this book is to help you learn about hunting with a muzzleloader. Whether you're new to muzzleloading, new to hunting, or experienced at both sports, this book will provide you with days afield with an old-style firearm that are more safe, successful, and enjoyable.

Muzzleloader hunting is one of the fastest-growing outdoor recreations in America. Rebirth of the rich heritage of hunting with primitive firearms began in the mid-1950s, when Turner Kirkland, Val Forgett, and a few others started marketing the first modern-made muzzleloaders in the United States. Ironically, Americans were inspired to join this age-old sport by the day's most modern technology—television, which brought the glamorized adventures of Davy Crockett to their living rooms. While the Davy Crockett fad faded, blackpowder shooting grew. Today it is bigger than ever, with dozens of companies making or marketing muzzleloaders and accessories. All but five states in the Union now conduct special muzzleloader-only hunting seasons each year.

An estimated 2 million shooters enjoy hunting with muzzleloaders today. Most continue to use modern guns, but many have converted completely to primitive arms. They are the ones who have become most infatuated with the romance and self-sufficiency of shooting with black powder, or the challenge and heritage in getting closer or shooting better—in other words, becoming better hunters.

There are many traditions connected with using primitive firearms. These customs vary slightly depending on the type and history of the muzzleloader being used, but the basics are the same. Some muzzleloading hunters use modern aids and adaptations to improve their hunting success; but, for many others, the real challenge is in doing things exactly the way their forefathers did them.

Hunting with a muzzleloader is demanding of the hunter because of range limitations and reloading times required. Accordingly, the hunter's attitude is crucial. In hunting with a muzzleloader, always think "hunting" instead of "shooting;" think "waiting" instead of "chasing;" think "patience" on your part.

The muzzleloader hunter accepts a challenge that carries a high degree of responsibility. Each shot is hand-loaded. The hunter must determine the effectiveness of a load (its reach, its punch, its suitability to the game, its effectiveness in a particular firearm) and ensure that it is correctly and safely put together in the gun time after time. Usually the muzzleloader hunter has the opportunity for just one shot. This means that a clean, decisive kill depends on making the single shot count.

Developing good loads, shooting ability, and awareness of shooting limits takes time and effort. There are no substitutes. Only those who are willing to invest themselves in learning and practice should pick up a muzzleloader for hunting. For those who are willing to accept the challenge and responsibility, rewarding and satisfying hours lie in store.

Part I
The Basics of Blackpowder Hunting

NRA Staff Photo

Part 2

The Basics of
Blackpowder
Handloading

Chapter 1

The Muzzleloading Firearm

The muzzleloading firearm offers the hunter a unique challenge and extra satisfaction that modern guns can't. The muzzleloader's one-shot challenge to marksmanship compels you to get close. Then you must depend on the accuracy and effectiveness of a load you've developed yourself. The feel of the gun and your skill in using it are things you share with generations of forefathers, elements that add to the enjoyment and satisfaction of hunting.

Photo by Mike Strandlund

The one-shot, short-range challenge of a muzzleloading firearm allows a sportsman to test the limits of his hunting skill.

The Elements of Muzzleloading

While the attractions and rewards of muzzleloading are complex, the guns themselves are quite simple. They consist of a barrel/breech assembly to hold the load and guide the projectile; a lock/trigger system to ignite the charge; sights for aiming; and the stock.

3

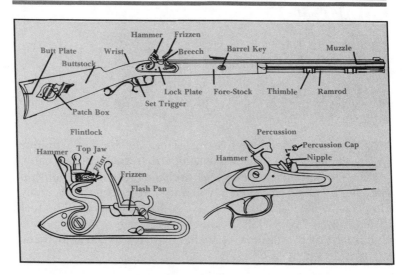

Muzzleloaders are distinguished from modern guns three ways. First, they are loaded by pushing the loose load components—the propellant and the projectile—down the barrel from the muzzle. The first component to be loaded is *black powder*, a term not meant to signify color but rather the name of a chemical mixture completely different from the smokeless powder used in brass cartridges and shotshells. This powder is ignited not by a self-contained primer, but by a percussion cap or a flint and priming powder.

Around this basic system many types of guns have been designed. The most basic, and most common, are the single-barrel firearms: muzzleloading rifles, muskets, shotguns, and pistols. There are a few models of each that have multiple barrels. The most complex muzzleloader is the revolver, a multi-shot gun with a cylinder magazine available in handguns and, rarely, carbines.

The Modern Hunting Muzzleloader

While a few traditionalists use authentic old-time muzzleloaders for hunting and target shooting, this usually isn't practical. Age and neglect have rendered most of the originals inoperative or unsafe; additional wear may hurt the value of a treasured antique.

A handful of American craftsmen build custom muzzleloaders, some from scratch, some from high-quality components. The firearms built by the most competent of these professionals are among the most revered of all guns made today.

Photo by Mike Strandlund

Muzzleloaders used by modern hunters come in a wide variety of designs. Two of the most popular blackpowder rifles are the mass-produced percussion gun (top) and the custom-made flintlock.

The great majority of blackpowder hunters today use contemporary-designed or replica muzzleloaders. A number of mass-produced models are made in America, and many are imported from Spain, Italy, and England. Their design, quality, and cost can vary greatly. The workings and appearance of some closely match the originals; others are thoroughly modern. It's a good idea to study the market and your needs thoroughly, then test-shoot a few guns before buying, to get the one that's right for you.

Ignition Systems

Muzzleloading firearms in use today utilize one of two methods to ignite the powder charge. These are either flint/priming powder ignition, or a percussion cap with a chemical compound that explodes when struck.

Ignition of the earliest firearms, invented just before 1400, was provided by a simple smoldering ember held to an open flash hole—similar to a primitive cannon. To make firearms practical for more than just point-blank shooting, gunsmiths needed a device that would ignite the powder without disturbing the shooter's aim. The first such device was a matchlock, a simple clamp holding a burning wick that could be lowered to the touch-hole by a lever. Next in the evolution of igniters was the wheel-lock—a mechanical device operating something like the wheel

5

FLINTLOCK   PERCUSSION

These diagrams depict the workings of flint and percussion ignition systems. With the flintlock (left), the cock holds a sharpened piece of flint, which is driven against the hinged steel frizzen when the trigger is tripped. The impact simultaneously snaps open the frizzen, exposing the priming powder and creating a spark. The spark ignites the priming powder, and the flame rushes through the open flash channel to ignite the charge. The percussion system (right) centers around a metal cap containing an explosive compound; it detonates upon impact of the hammer, shooting flame through a closed system comprised of a nipple and usually a hollow bolt called a bolster before it reaches the main powder charge.

of a modern-day cigarette lighter, which threw sparks onto a pan filled with priming powder. The wheellock was an improvement, but cumbersome and very expensive to make in pre-industrial times.

About 1615, the flintlock was invented. An ingeniously simple device that was state of the art for two centuries, the flintlock has a clamp that holds a piece of sharpened flint. When the trigger is pulled, the flint strikes sharply against a piece of steel and throws sparks into a priming pan. The priming powder ignites and sends flame through a flash channel to set off the main charge.

It wasn't until 1807 that inventors improved upon the flintlock ignition system. The new system was the percussion cap, which made ignition faster and more reliable. The percussion cap contains a small charge of fulminate of mercury, which detonates when struck by the hammer. Flame from the cap travels through a nipple and flash channel to ignite the main charge.

Percussion caps replaced flint as shooters found they were more dependable; they provided a surer spark, there were fewer moving parts in the lock, and the flash channel was a closed system, which helped keep moisture away from the powder charge in wet weather.

The percussion cap slowly replaced flint ignition systems and became the predominant ignition type in the mid-1800s. Many flintlock rifles were converted to percussion during this time. The cartridge gun became the preferred firearm in the later 1800s, though many percussion and some flintlocks remained in use.

Today, the great majority of muzzleloader hunters use the percussion cap. Its dependability and accuracy resulting from faster lock times is a definite advantage for most hunters. Those who use flintlocks do so for the challenge of making the shot, the satisfaction of using a more primitive method, or in the case of Pennsylvania, because only flintlocks are allowed during the muzzleloader hunting season.

Muzzleloader Designs

Muzzleloading firearms have been made in many designs and styles throughout their history. There have been long guns and carbines, stocks cut to fit against the shooter's upper arm, stocks cut with a shallower curve to fit against the shoulder, and even rounded stocks meant to be held away from the body. Thick butts were made to allow the gun to be used as a club in hand-to-hand combat; narrow butts allowed for lighter handling and elegance. Gun stocks from butt to lock have been shaped in sleek straight lines, full rounded curves, and every contour in between. The length of the stock has varied as well, some extending to just in front of the trigger guard, others running the entire length of the barrel. Carving is often used to give beauty and personality to the wooden parts.

Photo by Rick Hacker

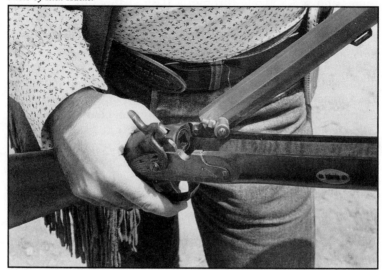

Photo by Dwain Bland

An array of distinctive features have been built in the muzzle-loader through the years, some for function, some for decoration. A pragmatic hunter might want a rather plain-looking gun with convenience features like a quickly detachable barrel. A shooter enamored by the romance of black-powder guns might take a fancy to antiquated brass adornments.

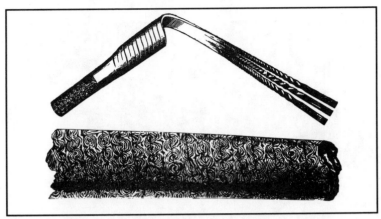

Old-time Damascus barrels were made by twisting ribbons of iron and steel around a pipe and hammer-welding them together. These barrels are of relatively weak design and may have been further weakened by time and neglect. Their use is not recommended.

The lock and other metal parts (often called a gun's "hardware") have been made of iron, brass, silver, nickel, gold, ivory, and alloys of varied composition. The metal is often used to combine decorative effect with usefulness in patchboxes, lock plates, and ramrod thimbles. In other components, such as nose caps and buttplates, beauty and protection are combined. Other variations are solely for looks, such as intricate precious metal inlays, or solely for function. On military weapons, metal bands are often incorporated to provide additional strength.

Barrels come in diverse styles, as well. The single barrel with a single lock is the most common. Double-barrel guns have been made throughout the muzzleloader's history, and are likely to be side-by-side in construction with individual locks for each barrel. Double-barrels are available in rifles, smoothbores, and combinations for flexibility of firepower. More rare are double barrels in an over/under position.

The outside configuration of a gun barrel can be round, octagonal, or octagonal on the breech end and round near the muzzle. The thickness of the barrel walls also varies and affects the weight of a firearm. This thickness may be the same throughout the length of the barrel, tapered at the muzzle end, or "swamped" to be smaller in the middle than at either end. A tapered or swamped barrel allows the gun maker to decrease the overall weight of the barrel while maintaining a heavier breech where pressures generated in firing will be greater.

Photo by Rex Thomas

In selecting a muzzleloader for hunting, a shooter has several factors to consider, including caliber, design, features, and price. If you're shopping for a used blackpowder gun, closely examine functioning and bore condition

If the hunter has a desire to use the same firearm for another shooting activity as well as hunting, other design factors become important. Battle re-enactors, for example, will want to choose a firearm that meets the specifications of their re-enactment group concerning authenticity and appropriateness to the time period portrayed. Target shooters will want to make sure that sights offer the best accuracy and conform to competition regulations.

Any firearm that goes into the field must be carefully checked for wear, rust, and malfunction. Part of the planning for a hunting trip includes being sure the firearm is clean and in good working condition. The lock must function smoothly and without wobbling, and the half-cock notch should be solid. Screws should be snug and the nipple or flint should be in excellent condition.

A firearm does not have to be new or of modern manufacture to perform well in the field. If you use an antique gun, take care that there are no weak places or deep pits in the bore, an obstruction, rust, or the like. Any original firearm should be checked by a blackpowder gunsmith for soundness at the breech before being fired or taken to the field. Weakening from rust is especially difficult to detect in a Damascus barrel, and the use of original Damascus steel barrels is not recommended, even when they look serviceable.

A gun that is used only for hunting can be modified in many ways to make it more useful in the field. New firearms are finished and displayed in stores so that they will attract attention and entice a buyer. The hunter who wants to use a gun for other purposes during the off-season (decoration, target competition, etc.) will want to be careful about keeping hunting alterations temporary or in conformance with regulations for other purposes. A gun used strictly for hunting, however, can have a sling mounted, the finish changed, and sights altered to fit the need.

The sight picture may be enhanced for variable light conditions by using a non-shiny paint to highlight the front sight. It's also a good idea to mark the sight positions so that any jostling or bumps in the woods won't mess up the sights without warning. Use a cold chisel or scribe to make a visible mark at the base of the fixed sight, front or rear.

With an adjustable rear sight, seal the adjustment screw with a drop of clear nail polish or Loc-tite to prevent any movement between sighting-in and the time of the crucial shot.

Many hunters obscure the shiny finish on their muzzleloader's wood and metal parts to make it less conspicuous to game animals. Brass decoration can be dulled by simply rubbing with a dirty cleaning patch. The shine is restored by buffing with any good brass polish. The stock and barrel can be warmed and coated with a thin layer of beeswax to reduce shine. This process not only gives a matte finish to the firearm, but helps protect the gun and gives it a very slight tackiness that enhances the hunter's grip on the stock. Shine is restored by buffing the wax coating later. For permanently dulling the barrel, use a matte-finish browning compound.

Firearm Fit

No matter what the style or quality of a firearm, it should fit the hunter. Fit is one factor in how accurately the hunter can shoot. The firearm must fit in several ways.

The distance from the buttplate to the trigger should be roughly the length of the shooter's forearm from the inside of the bent elbow to the bend of the trigger finger. When the gun is brought to the shoulder, the sight picture should line up with the shooter's eye without extensive head movement, and with the thumb of the trigger hand about an inch in front of the

NRA Staff Photo

Before buying any gun, check its fit under field conditions. A stock too long or short, or with too much drop or not enough, can affect your shooting accuracy and pleasure.

nose. Weight and length may conform to the overall size of the hunter, or match the hunting conditions. Many hunters believe shorter, lighter guns are best suited to long hikes and difficult terrain. Longer, heavier guns may be better in some cases because they have less recoil and can often be shot more accurately.

The effect of recoil can also be related to the shape of the stock, the height and shape of the comb, and the shape of the buttplate. How the cheekpiece fits the face and its angle change how recoil is felt by the shooter on the face. The width, curve and hardness of the buttplate will affect felt recoil.

The muzzle-heaviness of a long-barrelled gun may at first seem awkward, but give it a fair test to see if you can adapt to the difference in balance.

There is a muzzleloader to fit every hunter and most hunting situations. Finding the right combination may take some study, time, and experimentation. Experienced hunters agree the pleasure of using a good, well-chosen muzzleloading firearm is well worth the trouble it takes to find one.

Muzzleloading Rifles

The first practical hunting muzzleloaders were muskets. These smoothbore guns worked fine as shotguns—shooting charges of multiple pellets—but were comparatively ineffective for shooting single balls. They were slow and difficult to load, and accuracy was marginal at best.

Well before the settlement of America, European gunsmiths discovered the benefits of making rifled barrels. Rifling—spiraling grooves in the bore—cause the projectile to rotate laterally in flight. The effect of this rotation is to balance the imperfections of the projectile and cause it to fly straighter.

There were certain other problems with early rifles, however. For the rifling to impart spin on the ball, the grooves had to grip the ball tightly. This required that an oversize ball be ham-

Photo by Richard P. Smith   *Photo by Leonard Rue Enterprises*

Blackpowder hunters today find success with a variety of approaches, whether they use a modern method or more traditional guns, gear, and tactics.

13

mered down the bore, which made loading difficult and dangerous, and which deformed the projectile and hurt its accuracy.
For most practical purposes, early hunters and soldiers preferred
the musket.

In the early 1700s, American gunsmiths made their first major
contribution to firearms technology: the patched ball. This inno-
vation, first tried in Europe in the 1500s, was perfected by Ger-
man-American gunsmiths from southern Pennsylvania. Their
system combined the musket's ease of loading with the rifle's
accuracy.

The patched ball gun has a rifled barrel and shoots an undersized ball seated in a lubricated cloth patch. With their combined
width, the patching and the ball fit snugly in the bore; the rifling
grips the patch, and the patch grips the ball. The "give" in the
lubricated patch allows it to slide easily down the bore and protects the ball, so deformation by loading or by the rifling is
minimized.

This improved firearms technology made for a faster, more
accurate bullet, which was valued by frontiersmen whose lives
depended on their rifles.

In the mid-1800s, the conical bullet came under development.
Used in rifled military arms, the hollow-based minie-type balls
were easier to load than balls, formed a good pressure seal,
grabbed the rifling, and, once shot, retained energy better at
longer ranges than balls.

Today, hunters use both patched balls and conical bullets in
their rifles. The choice depends on personal preference or the
design of the rifle. Some manufacturers claim their barrels are
suitable for both, but generally the different types of projectiles
require different barrel configurations for best accuracy.

The barrel design is based mainly on the twist of rifling, in
terms of how many inches of barrel it takes for the rifling to
make one complete turn. Slow-twist barrels (one turn in 66-72
inches) are designed for round balls, while fast-twist (one turn
in 22 to 48 inches) is usually best for conicals. A slow twist is not
good for conicals because conicals need more spin for stability.
Many rifles made today have a one-in-48 twist, considered a
good compromise to handle both patched balls and conicals. The
depth that the rifling is cut into the bore, the distance between
grooves, and the number of grooves vary from one gun to
another. The depth of the rifling is the distance between the top
of the lands to the bottom of the grooves and is measured in

thousandths of an inch. The average rifling is cut between five and fifteen thousandths of an inch deep. Patched balls require a deeper rifling for a good grip on the patch. Conicals need fairly shallow rifling, which allows the soft lead to conform to the rifling grooves to make a good gas seal, but will not cut deeply into the bullets and harm their accuracy. Rifles designed to shoot patched balls usually have more grooves—four to eight— than guns made to shoot conicals, which usually have three or four grooves.

Choosing a Rifle

Your choice of rifle will depend on several factors: the type of game you wish to hunt, the type of projectile you want to shoot, the design of gun you prefer, and the quality you can afford. In muzzleloaders, the quality of design and workmanship varies greatly. Cheaper guns are often not the value they appear to be. Malfunctions and poor performance will at best deprive you of full satisfaction with the sport; at worst, endanger you or others.

A primary consideration in choosing a rifle is the caliber, which determines the gun's energy potential. A muzzleloader's caliber is determined by the bore diameter in inches measured at the lands. For example, a .50-caliber rifle is a half-inch across at the narrowest measure of the bore. Most muzzleloaders produced today are between .32 caliber and .58 caliber.

Hunters seeking small game like squirrels and rabbits find calibers of .32 and .36 more than adequate for the job. On medium-size game like coyotes, .45 caliber is a good choice. Roundball rifles of .50 caliber are ideal for hunting deer, while .54 should be considered minimum for elk-sized game and .58 caliber for anything bigger. Of course, the ultimate game-harvesting ability of your gun will be determined by your load and shot placement. Many states have minimum requirements for calibers and loads for big game muzzleloader seasons.

Among muzzleloading rifles, the basic designs are the long rifle, half-stock, military-style, and contemporary. The long rifle, the first all-American gun, is a replica of long-barreled, full-stock guns popular from the mid-1700s to the mid-1800s. The forestocks of these rifles run the full length of the barrel. They usually have a curved buttplate and brass hardware. Their long barrels are typically rifled with slow twists for patched balls. Sights fitted on long rifles tend to be fixed and rather crude. Long rifles are

Photo by Mike Strandlund

Photo by Dr. Sam Fadala

The overwhelming choices among modern muzzleloading riflemen are guns based on original designs. The two main variations on this theme are the full-stock rifle (above) and the half-stock Hawken type.

preferred mostly by eastern hunters who wish to relive the past of hunters in that area.

Half-stock rifles are by far the most popular blackpowder models today. They are replicas of the muzzleloading carbines that gained popularity in the Great Plains and West of the early 1800s. Many hunters find their shorter barrels easier to manage in the field.

Half-stock rifles, with their straight buttstocks and adjustable sights, are generally more practical for the average hunter. The least popular design among muzzleloading hunters is the military rifle. Patterned after guns like soldiers carried from the French and Indian War to the Civil War, these rifles sport massive stocks and hardware, though barrels are comparatively thin. Many are made for show—displays or battle re-enactments—and functionality is often marginal. Some guns in this class, however, are quite dependable and accurate. Most are bored in large calibers like .58. Designs range from bulky, musket-like pieces like the Enfield or Zouave rifles, to small carbines. While many guns of this style make fine hunting firearms, they are not popular among hunters because the caliber is overly large, the rifles are heavy, and hardware is excessive and nontraditional for hunting rifles.

Photo by Richard P. Smith   *Photo by Peter Schoonmaker*

Underhammer and sidehammer rifles have never been as popular as the traditional tophammer guns. The advantage of these uncommon designs is that repercussion from the cap is directed away from the shooter's face.

Photo Courtesy Navy Arms

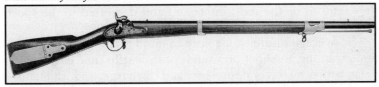

Military-style muzzleloaders have seen little use among hunters because of their bulk and overly large calibers. They can provide ample bullet energy and surprising accuracy, however.

Contemporary muzzleloaders are no-nonsense muzzleloaders with emphasis on function. They are unadorned, bearing a closer resemblance to a modern firearm than an old-time frontloader. While some are plain ugly in the eyes of most traditionalists, they are designed to get the job done well—usually for a minimum cost. Some contemporary muzzleloaders are equipped with modern features like scope mounts.

17

Photo by Dr. Sam Fadala

Contemporary-style muzzleloaders are built to get the job done with no nonsense. They lack frills but sport functional features like recoil pads, superior iron sights, and fast locks.

Rifle Features

Muzzleloading rifles have various features designed to add to the appearance or function of the gun.

One of the hunter's major considerations is the type of ignition he wants on his rifle. As discussed previously, the percussion cap is preferred by muzzleloading hunters who want the most in reliability and efficiency of operation. Flintlocks are favored by hunters who place more importance in doing it the old way. Ironically, flintlock hunters are often the most successful because they tend to be the most interested and dedicated to the sport and devote the most time to practice and hunting.

The average hunter must keep in mind that it takes conscientious training to shoot accurately with a rifle that has a slight delay between trigger depression and discharge, and which during that delay spews fire and smoke four inches from his face. He must be very detail-minded about maintaining a flintlock on the hunt, lest rain—even humidity or a breeze—render his ignition system useless and cost him an animal. Most experts recommend that a first-time muzzleloader hunter use a percussion gun.

Replicas often have brass adornments such as a fore-end cap and patch box. These are pretty, but may hurt your hunting success unless the brass is allowed to tarnish and stay that way. Reproductions may have other features made for looks rather than function; a curved, pointed metal buttplate may be pleasing, but only until it drives against your shoulder under force of a heavy hunting load.

Don't underestimate the importance of having good sights that enhance the accuracy of your style of shooting. The accuracy of any gun is only equal to that of its sights. Sights come in a variety of designs, usually emphasizing either shooting accuracy or historical accuracy, sometimes offering a compromise. Many replica rifles, long rifles especially, have fixed sights, as did the

Photos by Rick Hacker

Sights and triggers that are well-made and adjustable are definite aids to accuracy for the rifleman.

originals. Some of the blade-front/buckhorn-rear sights are difficult to align, are imprecise, and require tapping, filing, or change of hold for adjustment. There are, however, high-quality fixed sights designed for accuracy.

Most hunters have best luck with the adjustable target sights found on most contemporary and half-stock rifles. These sights typically have a wide blade or round bead atop a blade for a front sight, and graduated rear sights adjustable for windage

Photos by Richard P. Smith

Sighting with a blackpowder rifle can be more precise with a riflescope (not legal everywhere), or modifications can be made to sights such as painting the front sight white for visibility in low light.

and elevation. Some hunters have the best success with peep sights—a small aperture sight near the tang, replacing the more common buckhorn rear sight. While this is the most accurate setup for many shooters, some hunters have difficulty using them in the field, especially when trying to get on-target with obscured or moving game.

A disadvantage of adjustable sights is that some models are prone to being broken or knocked out of adjustment. The cheaper models comprised of several components may come apart if neglected or bumped sharply.

There are many styles of replacement sights available. If you are not satisfied with your rifle's factory sights, you can probably get better results with replacements. If practical, try before you buy.

Telescopic sights are seen occasionally on muzzleloaders, though they are illegal in many states. There's no doubt that they improve the accuracy of most shooters, but in the eyes of most muzzleloading hunters they defeat the purpose of hunting with a primitive firearm.

Photo by Mike Strandlund

Set triggers consist of a main trigger that releases the hammer, and a secondary trigger that "sets" the main trigger to lighten its pull. A set main trigger may improve accuracy under many conditions, but usually has such a light pull that it may trip prematurely in the excitement of the hunt.

Another feature found on many muzzleloader rifles is a set trigger. This consists of a double trigger; the rear trigger is first pulled to "set" the main trigger so it trips with very light pressure, which may help accuracy. The main trigger can also be tripped without being set, usually with considerable pressure. This system was developed primarily for target shooters, who fired under ideal, controlled circumstances. Its usefulness for hunters is questionable—it is easy to discharge the gun prematurely in an exciting shooting situation with the main trigger set. If you try to shoot the gun without setting the main trigger, the pull can be

21

Photo Courtesy Lyman Products

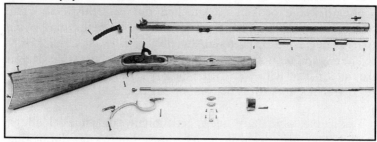

Many models of muzzleloaders can be purchased in easy-to-assemble kit form, which saves money and adds to the satisfaction of blackpowder hunting.

so great that it hurts accuracy. Most experienced muzzleloader hunters prefer single-trigger rifles.

Longer barrels provide a longer sighting plane, which may improve the shooter's accuracy. But with the long barrel's advantage comes the disadvantage of being more unwieldy. A shorter barrel helps when you have to shoot or reload quickly or in cramped quarters, and is easier to carry on a hard hike.

Along with the major differences in design among rifles are more subtle differences. Some rifle stocks have a considerable drop in comb, which places the barrel high in relation to the stock. This may affect shooting pleasure and accuracy. Normally, long rifles have a substantial drop in comb, which causes the shooter to shoot with his head in a more upright position. Half-stock, military, and contemporary rifles typically have straighter stocks, which require the shooter to shoot with his head lower.

Quality of workmanship and materials also varies considerably among muzzleloaders, old and new. A well-built barrel is the most accurate and safest. The locks of poor-quality guns are undependable, and the inletting of stocks is sloppy. Some rifles are built for looks, not function; they may be pretty and pretty expensive, yet not shoot as well as an inexpensive gun. Talking with owners (and former owners) of several makes of muzzleloaders will give you an idea of the quality and value of different makes of guns.

Original muzzleloaders, too, covered the spectrum of quality. Some were better than most made today; others, notably trade rifles, were of very poor quality. Most were built of steel quite soft by modern standards. Never shoot an original muzzleloader unless it has been checked carefully and test-fired by a competent gunsmith.

Many muzzleloaders sold today are also available in easy-to-assemble kit form. Using a rifle you finished yourself lends an extra sense of satisfaction complimentary to the sport. It can also save around 25 percent on the cost of the gun.

The Muzzleloading Shotgun

While the sport of muzzleloader hunting is growing in all areas, blackpowder shotguns have not enjoyed the popularity that their rifled counterparts have. The main reason is that while riflemen enjoy special seasons and certain advantages to hunting with muzzleloaders, there are no such benefits for the blackpowder shotgunner. Also, shotgunners typically shoot many more rounds than riflemen, and many seem deterred by the extra time and labor of reloading a blackpowder scattergun.

Hunters who take time to develop good loads for their blackpowder shotguns do find them quite efficient for hunting, however. They may be used in nearly any application suitable for a modern scattergun.

Most muzzleloading shotguns on the market today are 12-gauge guns, with some 10 gauges and a few smaller shotguns available. Inexpen-

Photo by Dwain Bland

A blackpowder shotgun may take some time to adjust to, but is capable of accuracy and energy approaching that of modern shotguns.

sive shotguns usually have an open choke, which limits their use on larger, longer-range game. The better guns often have choked muzzles, which are more expensive to manufacture. Modern muzzleloading shotguns are also available with screw-in muzzle inserts that can be interchanged to vary the choke.

The most popular guns of this category are side-by-side double-barrels. Several models of single-barrel shotguns are also manufactured, and some large-bore muskets also serve well as scatterguns. The selection of replica blackpowder smoothbores on the market is much more limited than rifles or handguns, proportional to their popularity. Original muzzleloading shotguns are available, but should be checked by a qualified gunsmith before they are test-fired. Even so, they should be used with relatively light loads because age may have made the steel brittle.

Shotguns have smooth barrels, devoid of rifling grooves. A barrel of modern manufacture is made of steel alloy and will function well for many years if it is cleaned and lubricated as the manufacturer recommends and used within the maker's guidelines.

Older barrels may be made by the Damascus method of wrapping an iron rod with iron-alloy wire or ribbon and welding the wrap with heat and hammering. The result is a forged barrel that may have an invisible pattern or a rippled, high-contrast pattern of outstanding beauty. Shotguns with Damascus barrels have premium value as antiques. As working firearms, Damascus-barrelled shotguns have drawbacks. Some were built with barrel weaknesses that will not hold up to long or hard use. Others have gone through hard times, and rust may have caused

Photo by Mike Strandlund

Most muzzleloading shotguns are side-by-side double-barrels, though single-barrels and a few over/unders are also available.

unevenness in the barrel strength. In addition, because of the pattern, these weaknesses may be difficult to detect, even by a competent gunsmith with modern technology. The safest course is to leave a Damascus barrel at home and avoid the risk of accidental injury and damage to a valuable antique.

Smoothbore stocks range from the short, round shape of a German fowling piece to the military shape of the Brown Bess musket. Many of the gentleman's fowlers are ornately decorated. Most of the shotguns of modern make are quite utilitarian, however, and resemble modern smokeless powder guns in shape, weight, and size.

The blackpowder shotgunner must generally restrict himself to only standard lead-pellet loads. With some exceptions, manufacturers generally advise that steel shot, required by the federal government for waterfowl hunting in many areas, not be used in their shotguns. Steel shot is likely to erode the barrel. It can score the bore and widen a choked muzzle, which may or may not harm the performance of the shotgun. If steel shot is used, it must be loaded inside a heavy plastic shot cup designed to protect the barrel.

Muzzleloading Handguns

Muzzleloading handguns have very limited use to the hunter. Their designers did not intend blackpowder pistols for hunting, but solely to give their user a bit of advantage over a sword-wielding adversary. Their comparatively low energy precludes responsible use on deer or anything bigger. Tiny, elusive small game targets are difficult to hit with handguns. Usually, blackpowder handguns are selected by a hunter as a novelty, not as an effective hunting tool. Yet, some hunters find that blackpowder pistols and revolvers suit their needs. If the shooter has gained proficiency through load workup and practice, the handgun can be a viable hunting tool for small and medium game. Squirrels and rabbits, still and close, are good targets. So is game that can be called in close, such as turkeys and predators. Varmints like woodchucks and ground squirrels can be approached to effective handgun range.

The overwhelming choice among muzzleloading handgun hunters are cap-and-ball revolvers. Built along the lines of early Colt and Remington models, these replicas can attain good accuracy if the shooter becomes proficient in their use. These handguns are built in many different styles. Like all muzzleloaders,

Photo by Rick Hacker

Blackpowder handguns are fun for plinking but have very limited use to the hunter. With a few exceptions, they have neither the energy for large animals nor the accuracy for small ones.

some are built more for looks than function. Handguns with a simple bead front sight and notched-hammer rear sight are much more difficult to shoot accurately than those with improved or adjustable sights. Brass-frame revolvers develop play and lose accuracy after much shooting. The Remington style, with a topstrap over the cylinder, is generally more rugged and accurate than the Colt design, which has an open-top cylinder. Cap-and-ball revolvers are manufactured domestically and abroad, and quality varies considerably.

One disadvantage of the revolver is that projectiles lose velocity because of the gap between the cylinder and the barrel. Closed-chamber pistols develop more energy than revolvers because there is no such pressure escape.

NRA Staff Photo

The two basic blackpowder revolver designs include the Colt style (top) and the Remington style, based on designs from the mid-1800s. The Remington, with its full frame, is generally considered more rugged and accurate.

Single-shot pistols of interest to the hunter are limited to the large frontier-replica pistols and target-style pistol most commonly in .45 and .50 calibers. While .45 caliber may be a suitable close-range deer rifle, pistols of this size do not have the energy or precise bullet placement of a rifle, and should never be used to hunt game of deer size or bigger. The .50 caliber, used with a conical bullet and substantial powder charge, is marginal for close-range deer hunting by proficient marksmen.

Blackpowder handguns are legitimate "backup" guns where legal, used at point-blank range to dispatch wounded big game.

CHAPTER 2

BLACKPOWDER LOAD COMPONENTS

O ne of the more enjoyable elements of hunting with a muzzleloader is the variety of loads you can develop and use for different types of game and different shooting requirements. In blackpowder shooting, there are no factory loads; each is a custom load you tailor to the situation at hand.

A muzzleloader load consists of four components: propellant or powder, projectile, primer, and buffer/lubrication material. These components must be selected and combined properly to ensure optimum accuracy, game-harvesting ability, and shooter safety.

Photo by Mike Strandlund

One of the joys of muzzleloader hunting is working up your own loads, experimenting with different powders, projectiles, and loading techniques, trying to glean the most accuracy and energy from your primitive firearm.

29

Muzzleloader Propellants

The traditional energy source for muzzleloaders is black powder, a chemical compound of sulphur, charcoal, and saltpeter. It propels a bullet or pellet charge by burning instantly, suddenly creating very high pressure behind the bullet and moving the projectile down the bore.

Black powder is a volatile propellant and loads that are too heavy or that create a barrel obstruction can cause a destructive breech explosion. Yet, black powder is not as potent as modern smokeless powder. Modern gunpowder has about three times the pressure potential of black powder, and using smokeless powder—even small quantities—will lead to probable gun destruction and possible injury. Use only powder in original cans labeled "black powder." The only alternative to black powder is a substance called Pyrodex, a brand name for a different chemical composition that has nearly identical burning and shooting traits as black powder. The main difference is that Pyrodex is a bit more difficult to ignite than black powder, so it is not recommended for use in flintlocks. Pyrodex also requires firmer packing than black powder for consistent burning.

Both black powder and Pyrodex are manufactured in a variety of granulations, each suited to different purposes. Powder of a finer granulation burns faster and creates somewhat more pres-

Photo by Rick Hacker

Only the correct amount and granulation of black powder or Pyrodex may be used in a muzzleloader. Improper loads or smokeless powder can be very dangerous.

sure in the breech of the gun. Higher pressure gives higher projectile velocity, but may hurt bullet or pellet performance and create a safety hazard.

Granulations of black powder are designated by a series of the letter F. More Fs mean finer powder. Black powder designated FFFFg typically called four-F) is the finest granulation. It is used exclusively as priming powder in the pans of flintlocks. FFFg (three-F) black powder is standard for all blackpowder pistols and small- and medium-bore rifles. It is recommended for most rifles up to and including .45 caliber, and for some .50-caliber rifles (check manufacturer's recommendations). FFg (two-F) powder is the standard for large-bore rifles, muskets, and shotguns. Fg (one-F) black powder, the coarsest available, is used in some large shotguns and muskets.

Pyrodex has a different labeling system, listing its three types of powder as RS (for rifle/shotgun), P (for pistol), and C (for cartridge). The RS granulation is the only type recommended for use in any rifles or shotguns.

NRA Staff Photo

Using Propellants

To manipulate the accuracy, noise, recoil, and game-taking ability of a load, the shooter tries different volumes and sometimes different types of powder, within certain parameters outlined for his gun and bullet type.

Blackpowder and Pyrodex are typically measured by volume, not by weight. Shooters use volume measures that approximate powder weights in grains. Target shooters sometimes weigh powder charges, but usually it isn't practical for hunters. Since Pyrodex is lighter than black powder, it

Use care in measuring and loading propellants, especially in the distracting conditions of hunting.

Photo by Mike Strandlund

Muzzleloader rifle projectiles come in a variety of designs with a wide range of energy, accuracy, and suitability for certain firearms.

should always be measured by volume to avoid a charge that is too potent. If you measure by volume, use the same volume of Pyrodex as black powder. Though the volumes will be the same and give approximately the same amount of energy, the Pyrodex will actually weigh less.

Always study recommendations of the gun manufacturer before experimenting with powder charges. Responsible manufacturers provide information on the proper powder type, suggested loads, and maximum loads.

Once you've determined the parameters of possible loads for your gun, you can begin experimenting with different charges. Information on load workup is found in Chapters 5 and 6.

Both black powder and Pyrodex should be stored in a cool, dry, secure place where they will not be subject to extreme temperature or moisture variations. Stored or in use, both types of powder should be away from any sources of ignition including cigarettes. If you smoke while hunting, put your rifle and powder container down at a safe distance.

Muzzleloader Projectiles

Standard muzzleloading rifle and pistol projectiles are pure lead, either round or conical, any of which may be referred to as balls or bullets. Shotgun pellets used in blackpowder guns are lead alloys identical to those used in modern shotshells.

The type of projectile you use will determine the accuracy, energy, and trajectory of your shots.

Muzzleloader projectiles work differently from modern bullets. All bullets down game by creating shock or blood loss, or disrupting the function of a vital organ. They do this by the energy of impact and penetration, which is created by the bullet's weight and velocity. Modern bullets derive most of their energy from very high velocity. In the energy formula, velocity is twice as important as weight, which is why centerfire bullets are more efficient than those from muzzleloaders.

Muzzleloader hunters who want maximum performance from their bullets must think in terms of bullet mass, retained energy, and expansion. To effectively incapacitate game, the bullet must be fired with sufficient energy and reach its target before losing too much of its initial energy. It must penetrate deeply, and expand or deform to create a large wound channel and transfer as much energy to the animal as possible. There are three basic types of projectiles available to the muzzleloading rifle hunter. They include the patched round ball, the solid-based conical bullet, and the hollow-based bullet.

Patched Ball

As explained in Chapter 1, the patched round ball is a bit smaller than the rifle's bore. It is held in a cloth patch that wraps around the rear half of the ball. The patch serves as a kind of gasket, sealing most of the gas pressure and allowing the rifling to put spin on the ball without gouging it.

Compared to conical projectiles, the patched ball generally has higher velocity and flatter trajectory at closer ranges. It can also generally be developed into a very accurate load provided the gun is high quality and designed for round balls. The major drawback of the round ball is its comparatively low energy and substantial drop at longer ranges. Round balls are considerably lighter than conicals of the same caliber. They are also less aerodynamic, affected more by air friction and draft. As a result, round balls start with less energy and lose energy faster than conicals propelled by similar powder charges.

Round balls may be made either by casting lead in a mold or by swaging—forming them by compression. Molded balls often have a deformity, called a sprue, caused by the inlet hole in the mold. This deformity has no effect on the flight of the ball—provided it is loaded correctly. The sprue must be up, facing out of the muzzle, as it is loaded. Contrary to common thought, a small deformity of the front of the projectile makes little or no difference in its flight, but deformity at the rear or sides may have a great effect.

The fit of the round ball in the rifle bore is important to accuracy and velocity. The ball should be about 5 to 10 thousandths of an inch smaller than the diameter of the bore. Bore sizes and ball sizes vary somewhat by manufacturer; shooters must often experiment to find the right fit. If the patched ball will slip very easily into the bore, it is too loose; if you must hammer it to get it seated on the powder, it is too snug. Try a different size ball or patch.

The functions of the patch are to hold the ball firmly, seal most of the gases to maximize velocity, and lubricate the bore for easier loading and more consistent shooting. The patch is crucial to the performance of a round ball.

Patches are subjected to tremendous forces, so they must be tough. A hardy cloth such as pure cotton or linen is among the best. Polyester/cotton blends are not satisfactory because they melt, fouling the bore. Patches must also be lubricated to facilitate loading and to help form a better seal. Though some shooters use saliva, oil-based lubricants are best. Grease or oil keeps the patch from drying out in long days afield. Prelubricated patches are also available.

The patch lube you use for hunting must perform well under the temperatures that may be encountered when hunting. The lube's reaction to varying temperature is far more critical for the hunter than for a target shooter. Some grease-base lubes get stiff and are extremely hard to load in cold weather. Liquid lubes may freeze. You may risk breaking a ramrod, particularly if the ball gets stuck part way down the barrel. Normally, hot weather is not a problem, though some grease-base lubes can become runny when the temperature rises. Try several different lubes at the range to see which performs the best. Store some overnight in the refrigerator and see if that affects its loading characteristics. It is far better to find this out before you need a quick second load in the field. Also, be consistent when applying lube to the patches, particularly for hunting purposes. Soak it thoroughly in the lubrication, then remove the excess so the patch is not "wet." Don't get the patch so greasy or wet that lubricant will soak into the powder charge. Experiment with different types of lubricant—commercial brands, shortening, and water-soluble oil.

For best accuracy, most shooters find they must employ patched balls that fit the bore very tightly, to the point that they may be hard to load. The condition of the bore is also important in patched ball accuracy. It must not be rusted, pitted, or otherwise rough, or it will grab the patch and shoot inconsistently.

There are a couple of tests you can perform with your patched ball load to see if it is right. Load a ball/patch combination in a clean, unprimed gun, then remove it with a ball puller. The

Photo by Mike Strandlund

Photo by Mike Strandlund

To determine the quality of your patching material, retrieve a patch that has been shot downrange and inspect it for tears and scorches. A good patch will be intact after the shot.

patch should not be torn or show signs of almost tearing. The pattern of a rough-texture patch should be imprinted on the circumference of the ball where it contacted the bore wall. After this test, shoot a test load and retrieve the patch, which can be found five or 10 yards downrange. The patch should have a gray ring where it contacted the bore, with lines that match the rifling. It should still show no signs of damage, especially smoldering or tears. A patch that makes a tight fit and holds up throughout the loading and firing process ensures that the forces affecting the ball are consistent, which is the key to round ball accuracy. Good accuracy can generally be achieved with round balls, though they do not have as much energy as conical bullets.

Solid-Base Conical

The solid-base conical is an elongated projectile with two or more bands slightly larger in diameter than the main body of the bullet. As the projectile is loaded, the rifling sculpts into these bands; the bullet turns with the rifling down to the powder upon loading and back out upon firing.

The bands form grooves that are filled with a thick lubricant before loading. The lubricant makes loading easier, keeps the bore cleaner, minimizes lead build-up in the rifling, and increases bullet velocity. Conical bullets with deep grease grooves provide lubrication for the entire length of the barrel upon firing, and are generally considered superior to those with shallow grooves.

These bullets offer good hunting accuracy, though they do not usually give the precise accuracy that patched balls can achieve. While spherical balls can be made close to perfect in

35

Photo by Mike Strandlund

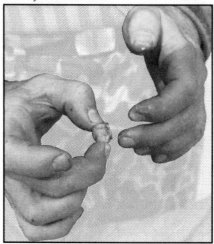

Maxi bullets must be lubricated with a grease-base substance for easier loading, consistent bore travel, and less fouling.

dimension and balance, longer bullets do not have such a perfect center of balance. There may be uneven pressures on the conical as it is fired, and the rifling scars on its circumference add to the imbalance. The faster rifling of guns designed for conicals helps stabilize them; they are accurate enough for close-range hunting of big game, but most squirrel hunters prefer the precision of patched balls.

Trajectory also affects how accurately a hunter can shoot conicals. The trajectory depends on the comparative weight of the projectile to its velocity. Conicals, being heavier and generally slower than a round ball, will drop more on their way to the target. A slight yardage miscalculation at longer ranges can cause a miss. Also, the greater the drop of a bullet, the more deviation there will be in that drop from shot to shot.

The main advantage of the conical is its higher level of retained energy. Bullets that are long in relation to their diameter have better aerodynamics and do not lose velocity as quickly as shorter bullets. Since a round ball is the shortest practical projectile, it is the *worst* as far as retaining energy. Longer bullets are much better. In a typical load, a patched ball will have only about one-third of its muzzle energy remaining after 100 yards. A typical conical load will have about half of its energy left in the same distance.

Solid-base conicals are popular among hunters because of their retained energy and the impact performance of some of the better designs. While both round balls and pointed solid bullets often drive straight through game without expansion unless they hit bone, some conicals have better results on muscle and vital tissue. The best performance usually comes from hollow-point and flat-nose designs. Testing a variety of designs by firing them into wet paper or clay will indicate which gives the best results for your gun, load, and effective range.

Minie Ball

While the patched ball and the solid-base conical have about equal popularity, the minie ball lags behind them in use by muzzleloading hunters. Developed by French Army Captain Claude Minie in the mid-1800s, the minie is a hollow-based conical that, like the patched ball, is slightly smaller than the bore diameter. The minie uses no patch, however; it depends on the powder ignition to flare its thin tail-end "skirt," which then engages the rifling and starts the bullet spinning as it travels down the bore.

The minie is generally less suitable than the other options for the average hunter, for two reasons. There are more factors affecting the accuracy of the minie, requiring very careful load workup. Also, the design of the minie can lead to problems in a hunting situation; its loose fit in the bore can cause it to move away from the powder charge, destroying accuracy and causing a safety hazard.

If you do use the minie, build loads carefully based on manufacturer recommendations. A fairly precise powder charge is required to get the right amount of flare from a certain bullet type in a certain gun. Too much flare or too little, and bullet impact will be inconsistent.

Minie balls must be lubricated on their outside, and the hollow base is often filled with grease. Grease residue on the flying projectile's base can affect accuracy, however, so some shooters use gas-seal wads with minie balls.

Muzzleloading Sabots

The muzzleloader hunter can also use modern semi-metal-jacketed bullets if he employs a sabot. A muzzleloader sabot (pronounced suh-*bow*) is a plastic sleeve that contains a smaller-diameter bullet inside a larger bore. The sabot fills the entire width of the bore, sealing gasses behind the fired bullet, engaging the rifling to spin the bullet, and peeling away from the bullet as it leaves the muzzle.

Photo by Mike Strandlund

Some muzzleloader hunters have had success with a plastic sabot (not legal everywhere) used with an undersized modern pistol bullet. The sabot fills the space between the bore and the smaller-diameter bullet, sealing gas and imparting spin on the projectile.

Modern rifle bullets are generally too long to use in a muzzleloading sabot. The most common way of employing sabots for muzzleloader hunting is with undersized pistol bullets. For example, a hunter with a .50-caliber rifle shoots a bullet of about .44 caliber, and a hunter with a .45-caliber rifle shoots a bullet of about .357 caliber, each contained in the proper size sabot.

The use of this system is relatively new, and hunters who have used them on game report varying success. A lighter, hollowpoint bullet fired with a sabot has a higher initial velocity, less medium-range trajectory, and better expansion than most common muzzleloader projectiles. Retained energy downrange is usually less, however, and sabots may have poor accuracy in some rifles.

Shooters who elect to use sabots must be very careful to watch for plastic build-up in the bore. Sabots may melt somewhat and leave plastic residue, which must be removed by brushing. If it is not, the deposits may prevent proper bullet seating and cause a breech explosion. A sabot may also creep forward of the powder charge if the gun is jarred. The warranties of at least one gun manufacturer exclude the use of sabots.

Shotgun Projectiles

Shotguns are loaded with a charge of dozens, even hundreds of pellets, rather than a single projectile. When shot at hunting yardages, these pellets form a pattern of two feet or more in diameter that makes it easier for the shooter to hit a small or moving target.

Pellets used in muzzleloading shotguns are the same as those used in modern shotshells. Pellet sizes range from buckshot, used on deer, to pellets barely as big as grains of sand, used for small gamebirds and target shooting.

Because the powder and pellets are loaded in loose charges, the loads must be plugged in place with material called wads and cards. A heavy wad, maybe with a card, between the powder and pellets keeps the two separated, and keeps the pellets from being badly deformed upon discharge. Another thin wad, or card, must be seated on top of the pellet charge to keep the pellets from sliding out of the barrel.

More information on shotgun pellets and loading can be found in Chapter 6.

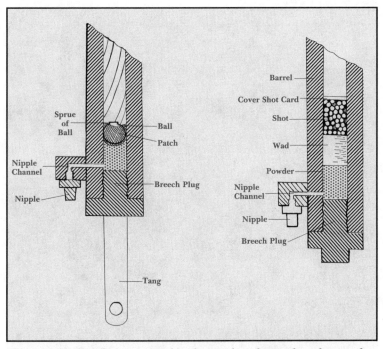

The round ball (left) is wrapped in the patch and seated on the powder, with the sprue pointed upward. The shotgun charge (right) contains powder separated by the pellet charge by a thick wad, with a thin card over the top to hold all components in place.

Ignition Systems

Your muzzleloader's ignition system may seem like the most minor component of the load chain, but it is actually the most important. Hunters who take their flint or cap for granted are courting disaster in terms of a ruined opportunity. Your effort, shooting accuracy, and hunting skill add up to nothing if your primer fails.

Flintlocks

The flintlock is a much more primitive ignition system than the percussion cap. While not as dependable as percussion, it can be quite reliable and efficient with a conscientious approach.

The flintlock is beautifully simplistic. It consists of three main parts: cock, pan, and frizzen. The cock or hammer is actually a clamp that holds a piece of sharp flint in a leather pad. The pan lies just below the flash channel, which is a small hole drilled into

Photo by Jenny Workosky

Until the shooter gets used to it, the fire and smoke spewed just inches from the face can be a major obstacle to accuracy with a flintlock. It is also a reason why shooters should wear safety glasses.

the breech, and holds the priming powder. The frizzen is an L-shaped, hinged steel plate that provides spark and protects the priming powder prior to the shot.

The flintlock is carried with the frizzen down and covering the priming powder. When the trigger is pulled, the cock thrusts the flint against the frizzen, simultaneously pushing it back to expose the powder and creating a shower of sparks. The sparks ignite the priming powder, shooting flame through the flash hole to the main charge.

The obvious concern with flintlocks is that by modern standards, there is a lot going on between the time you squeeze the trigger and the bullet leaves the muzzle. There can be a considerable time lapse during which the shooter must consciously maintain his aim, and there are several things that can go wrong.

The long ignition time lapse and malfunctions can be avoided by priming the pan carefully. Only very dry FFFFg blackpowder should be used. The equivalent of a "pinch" is about average, but don't actually pinch it—moisture from your hands may delay ignition. Pour it directly from a small container used just for pan priming.

The powder should lie on the pan, slanting to the bottom of the flash hole. The powder must not plug the flash hole or ignition will be delayed.

To light the priming powder reliably, the flint must throw a strong shower of sparks directly on the pan. The flints used for guns are square with a bevel on one edge of the forward side. The flint may be secured with bevel up or down; either may give best results, depending on the gun. The flint must be kept sharp by knapping—striking the leading edge with a small hammer. The forward edge of the flint should be parallel with the frizzen so the full length of the edge strikes the frizzen. The flint should be long enough to keep the top of the hammer from striking the frizzen, but not so long that the flint touches the frizzen when the hammer is on half-cock. This will expose the priming powder slightly, allowing it to spill or become moist.

For the flintlock hunter, keeping the priming powder dry is of the utmost concern. In rain or snow, moisture will invariably find its way to the priming powder. Even in very humid weather, the tendency for black powder to attract moisture will eventually render the prime useless. Use a lock cover on damp days. Whenever you hunt with a flintlock, examine the priming powder periodically. If it shows slight signs of becoming caked, replace it, with special care to remove powder in the flash hole with a wire.

Caplocks

Because of their better reliability, percussion cap systems, commonly called caplocks, are more popular than flintlocks. There are four sizes of caps available, but the great majority of muzzleloaders accept the number 11, a medium size.

The percussion cap is a small charge of chemical explosive held in a light metal cup that fits snugly over a tapered steel nipple. When the hammer drops, the priming mixture detonates and sends flame through a hole in the nipple and into the breech to the powder charge, usually by way of a drum, or hollow bolt, on the side of the barrel.

There are several things that can go wrong along the way. If the hammer does not fall squarely on the cap, it may not strike hard enough to detonate the primer mixture. The channel from the cap to the main powder charge must be completely clear of obstructions, including oil, or the fire may not reach the powder. Some caps are just plain duds, while others may be too weak to set off the powder, especially Pyrodex or damp black powder. Some weak caps are unreliable because of the gun's design; the flame from the cap is usually required to make a 90-degree turn, sometimes two, on its way to the powder charge.

There are ways of minimizing the chances of these ignition system failures. First, wipe all oil, dirt, and dampness from the breech (by way of the muzzle) and from the flash channel before loading. Remove the nipple, and perhaps the drum's clean-out screw, and use a pipecleaner or similar implement to clear any possible foreign debris. Before loading, snap a cap or two, holding the gun's muzzle a couple inches from a leaf. If you have a clear flash channel, the force of air from the muzzle should move the leaf visibly. (After you do this, check to ensure that cap debris has not clogged the nipple.)

Special cap and nipple designs can ensure the hottest possible spark. Some caps are hotter than others, though their potency is limited because of the hazard of outside-the-gun explosion. With too much explosive, the guns' hammer could blow back and shrapnel from the cap could fly. High-performance nipples are designed for a more directed flash and also have safety features to limit backpressure. These special nipples are recommended whenever Pyrodex is used.

Hunting Loads

How do muzzleloaders stack up in hunting situations? If you're switching from a centerfire rifle, there are definite differences. Velocities are lower. Calibers and bullet weights are larger than those used by modern centerfire rifles. What you lose in velocity you make up in larger caliber, heavier bullet weight, and closer shooting range. Accuracy varies from rifle to rifle, but at muzzleloading ranges the difference is not substantial. Maximum hunting ranges for a muzzleloader are around 40 to 80 yards for big game, 20 to 40 for small game. After the hunter's shooting ability, the most limiting factor is the fact that there is only one shot. A muzzleloader challenges the hunter to improve hunting skills, and can be a source of increased satisfaction when game is taken cleanly.

Different rifles will produce minor variations in velocity when using the same powder charge. Flintlocks and caplocks may also produce slightly different velocities with the same powder charge. These variations are insignificant provided the rifle chosen safely handles a strong load that produces consistent accuracy.

There is a definite difference in trajectory and velocity between the round ball and long bullets. Generally, round balls give a higher velocity and a flatter trajectory because of their lighter weight. Lyman's Black Powder Handbook is an excellent resource for muzzleloader hunters who are interested in ballistics. A fairly strong load in a .50-caliber rifle might produce 1,800 feet per second with a round ball and 1,400 fps (feet per second) with a bullet. Drop at various ranges would be as follows:

BULLET DROP AT VARIOUS RANGES					
(SOURCE: LYMAN BLACK POWDER HANDBOOK)					
	VELOCITY	50 YDS	75 YDS	100YDS.	125 YDS	150 YDS
ROUND BALL	1800 fps	2"	4"	8"	14"	23"
BULLET	1400 fps	3"	6"	11"	19"	29"

The chart shows why ranges under 100 yards should be the limit for most muzzleloader hunters. Individual shooting skill also limits most hunters to the 40- to 80-yard range. The adrenaline rush experienced when sighting a large buck does nothing for most hunters' shooting accuracy. Muzzleloader projectiles also develop greater lateral drift in a cross wind than center-fire bullets. Eight inches of drift in a moderate wind at 100 yards is common. Using the velocities shown above, comparative energies are shown for different caliber of round ball and bullets.

ROUND BALL ENERGY AT VARIOUS RANGES
(SOURCE: LYMAN BLACK POWDER HANDBOOK)

CALIBER ROUND BALL	VELOCITY	WEIGHT	ENERGY AT 50 YDS.	ENERGY AT 75 YDS.	ENERGY AT 100 YDS.
45	1800 fps	133 GRAINS	502 ft.-lbs.	362 ft.-lbs.	287 ft.-lbs.
50	1800 fps	180 GRAINS	736 ft.-lbs.	546 ft.-lbs.	431 ft.-lbs.
54	1800 fps	220 GRAINS	966 ft.-lbs.	731 ft.-lbs.	575 ft.-lbs.

CONICAL BULLET ENERGY AT VARIOUS RANGES
(SOURCE: LYMAN BLACK POWDER HANDBOOK)

CALIBER CONICAL	VELOCITY	WEIGHT	ENERGY AT 50 YDS.	ENERGY AT 75 YDS.	ENERGY AT 100 YDS.
45	1400 fps	230 GRAINS	633 ft.-lbs.	528 ft.-lbs.	457 ft.-lbs.
50	1400 fps	370 GRAINS	1063 ft.-lbs.	906 ft.-lbs.	789 ft.-lbs.
54	1400 fps	410 GRAINS	1350 ft.-lbs.	1194 ft.-lbs.	1071 ft.-lbs.

Both round balls and bullets are very effective game harvesters at close range. If elk- and bear-size game are being hunted, serious consideration should be given to the conical bullet because of its greater weight and penetration in heavy muscle mass.

Muzzleloaders do require some different perspectives on hunting techniques. Think caliber rather than velocity; think stalks over long shots. Think proper set-up for the first shot versus multiple shots. Hunting with a muzzleloader may also involve some tough decisions to pass up shots that would be easy with a centerfire rifle. One of the keys to success in any undertaking is confidence in yourself and your equipment. A muzzleloader is an open invitation to improve both your shooting and hunting skills.

CHAPTER 3

MUZZLELOADER HUNTING ACCESSORIES

Blackpowder hunters like to make things difficult for themselves. While modern guns are much easier to load, shoot, and maintain, a large measure of enjoyment can be derived from using the equipment necessary to hunt with a muzzleloader. As you accumulate and become skilled with using blackpowder gear, you'll add excitement and enjoyment to an already exciting, enjoyable sport.

Many muzzleloading accessories have been passed down from our pioneer ancestors. But the growing popularity of muzzleloading has resulted in an array of new gadgets never found in Daniel Boone's possibles bag.

Equipment used by the blackpowder hunter can be categorized as shooting gear, muzzleloader hunting accessories, maintenance supplies, clothing, general hunting aids, and woodsmanship gear.

Photo by Mike Strandlund

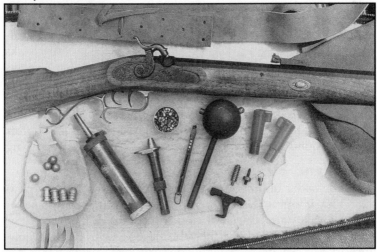

The muzzleloader hunter needs an array of shooting supplies as well as hunting and woodsmanship gear. The right equipment can make your hunt more safe, fun, and successful.

45

Shooting Gear

Photo by Rick Hacker

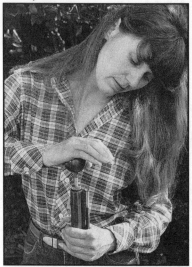

The short starter is a stubby, ball-handled ramrod that helps you start the bullet down the bore.

Ramrods

Most muzzleloading rifles come with a wooden ramrod. But wood can break under repeated use, and under these conditions, metal rods are more durable. To avoid damage to the muzzle, which can destroy the accuracy of the gun, you should always use a brass muzzle guard with steel ramrods. Most steel ramrods disassemble into three pieces for ease in carrying. Fiberglass rods are also available, and are nearly unbreakable. Some experts discourage their use because they are abrasive.

Short Starter

This is a six- to-eight-inch ramrod that helps get the bullet past the muzzle and starts it down the bore. While not always needed, it is essential for safe and efficient loading of conicals and tightly patched round balls.

Horns and Flasks

A muzzleloader hunter needs a container to carry his black powder. This is often the original one-pound can, but a smaller quantity is all that is needed, and is more convenient to carry. Metal powder flasks have the advantage over traditional powderhorns in having a spring-loaded closure. Powderhorns are traditional and often very artistic. With the advent of modern speedloaders, most blackpowder shooters do not actually hunt with the horn, since it can get in the way. Blackpowder shooters should never pour blackpowder directly from either horn or flask into the muzzle, but should use the powder measure or container of premeasured powder. Flasks or horns with a built-in measure on the tip are dangerous to use, because the entire contents could be set off by a spark.

NRA Staff Photo

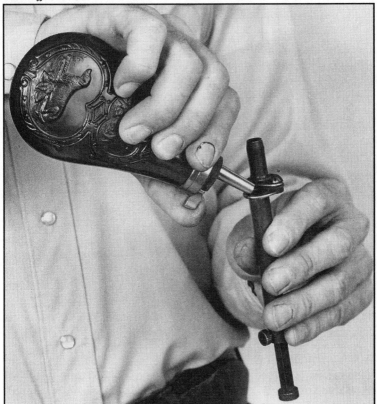

A blackpowder hunter needs a flask to carry powder and a measure to meter the right charge.

Powder Measure

A graduated powder measure is crucial for consistency and for developing accurate loads. Many have pour spouts or funnels attached to minimize powder spillage. Most are adjustable, measuring a volume of powder that approximates what that volume would weigh—usually from 10 to 120 grains. Measures are usually made of brass. If you use another type of measuring tool, be sure it is not made of steel, which can spark on contact with other metal and detonate any nearby powder.

Pan Charger

Photo by Bob Lollo

The primer, or charger, is a small powder container that dispenses a small amount of powder that may or may not be premeasured. It is the surest way for a flintlock shooter to carry priming powder and place the proper amount of powder in the pan. Old-time charging horns were made from the tip of a horn boiled and flattened to fit into the hunting bag, or from a hollowed-out antler.

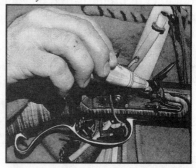

A pan charger, often made from a horn tip, is used to carry and dispense priming powder for flintlocks.

Capper

NRA Staff Photo

For percussion rifles and pistols, the capper makes it easier to put the cap on a nipple, especially when the shooter is wearing gloves. Be sure you have a capper that fits the caps for your rifle. Some cappers consist of a wheel of leather with holes punched around the edge and others are made of brass and hold 20 to 30 caps in a line. Magazine-style cappers hold a larger number of caps and are grav-

To keep caps organized and easier to install, many blackpowder shooters use a capper.

ity-fed. Cappers are also a good way to carry caps in one place and keep them from scattering around in your shooting bag.

Powder Can Spouts

These spouts, or funnels, fit over the mouths of blackpowder or Pyrodex containers. They make it easier to fill your flask, horn, or measure without spilling.

Ball Puller

This is a screw that fits on the end of your ramrod, used to remove a ball from the barrel of your gun by screwing directly into the lead ball. It's handy in case of a misfire or when you load a ball and forget to put powder behind it. The ball puller looks like a large sheetmetal screw with a brass washer attached to keep it centered in the barrel. A T-handle, attachable to your ramrod, makes ball pulling much easier. The ball puller can be dangerous to use. Experts recommend working some fine powder behind the charge and shooting the load out, rather than using a ball puller. Another method is to use one of the commercially available compressed-air tools for propelling the load.

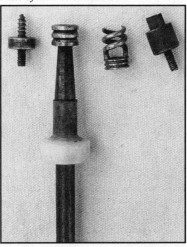

Photo by Mike Strandlund

A necessary accessory for the serious muzzleloader hunter is a stout workrod and variety of tips. Tips shown include, left to right: ball puller, cleaning jag, worm, and breech scraper.

Patch Knife

A patch knife or small pocketknife is used when shooting a round ball. It trims the patch material at the muzzle so the load can slide easily down the bore. Precut, round patches for shooting will eliminate the need for a patch knife, and also come prelubricated.

Nipple Pick

A wire pick is used to keep the nipple or channel between flash pan and the powder charge open. It is especially helpful on dry days when black powder or its residue cakes up, or on damp days when it soaks up moisture and clogs the breech area.

Knapping Hammer

A knapping hammer is helpful to flintlock shooters to flake away chips and make a sharp edge on their flints. These hammers are normally brass and often have a small screwdriver forged into the handle.

Photos by Mike Strandlund

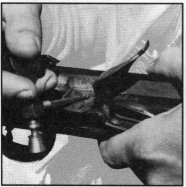
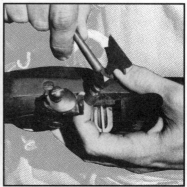

A handy tool for the flintlock shooter is this combination hammer and pick, used to knap the flint and keep the flash hole clear. This tool also has a small hatchet head.

The percussion gun shooter should always carry a nipple wrench to replace faulty nipples and unplug clogged flash channels.

Nipple Wrench

Caplock shooters should carry a nipple wrench in case the nipple must be removed for cleaning or when the flash channel needs to be cleared of debris.

Bullet Bag

A small bag for carrying projectiles also serves as a dispenser. Most consist of two pieces of leather sewn together to be carried inside the shooting bag. Soft lead has a way of picking up grit and impurities and the ball bag helps eliminate the problem.

Shot Container

The shot flask is used for carrying pellets for a blackpowder shotgun. Its measuring spout measures out the proper shot charge and inserts it into the bore.

Bullet Patches

Patching material should be a natural fabric such as cotton or linen and should be consistent in both thickness and weave. Pillow ticking, available in many fabric stores, is a good substitute, but normally this material needs to be washed to remove the sizing.

Lubricants/Prelubed Patches

A variety of lubricants is available for lubricating patches. Saliva or animal fat was used in the old days, but saliva contains salt and other chemicals that may harm the bore in time. Beware of products with low melting points that can seep into your powder and render it useless. Prelubricated patches used for shooting eliminate the need for lubricants in the shooting bag.

Tool Boxes

Photo by Mike Strandlund

Since you won't need to carry everything you need to maintain your blackpowder fire-arm into the field, a simple tool box will be useful. In it you can keep the equipment you need to fully clean your rifle, shotgun or pistol, a small mainspring vise, and extra tools such as screwdrivers, small hammers, wire brushes, locking pliers, and extra cleaning equipment.

Extra Parts

Muzzleloader hunters should always prepare for equipment breakdowns and malfunctions, and consistent with this, should carry as many spare parts as is reasonable.

For extended trips, it's a good idea to carry as many tools and shooting supplies as is reasonable in a sturdy tool chest.

Among the parts most apt to have problems are the priming system components—especially the flint or nipple. Carry extras.

Many muzzleloader hunters begin by replacing their standard nipple with a modified type that produces an extra hot flash, which greatly reduces the chance of a caplock misfire. The original muzzleloader hunters often carried an extra lock for their guns, in case of malfunction. This is still a good idea. A spare ramrod, particularly one that is metal and breaks down into several parts that screw together, is another good idea, since it doesn't take up much space. Flexible rods used to clean modern rifles and shotguns work on muzzleloaders too, if the proper rod tip accessories will adapt, and one in your cleaning kit can come in handy.

Muzzleloader Hunting Accessories

Along with his shooting supplies, the muzzleloader hunter can use some other firearm accessories to aid his hunting. They help prevent firearm malfunctions afield, make it easier to carry and care for the gun, or increase a hunter's chance of success.

Gun Covers and Protectors

Covers and protectors will help shield against the number one enemy of the blackpowder hunter: moisture.

A small piece of rubber tubing, sealed on one end, can protect the nipple on a caplock from getting wet, and if made correctly, act as a safety device. Some hunters waterproof their caplock nipple by sealing the cap with clear nail polish after it has been placed. On flintlocks, a coating of a mixture of thick grease and beeswax applied to the pan after charging can help keep the powder dry. Put a small bead of this mixture around the edge of the pan, then close the frizzen on this bead of grease.

Both flintlocks and caplocks will benefit from a fairly close-fitting leather cover that goes around the entire lock mechanism and covers part of the barrel. It should be liberally coated with oil or other waterproofing material. Plastic lock covers are excellent protectors, and in the early morning dew or in a drizzle, a wool gun cover that comes just past the lock is also helpful. A toy balloon or piece of plastic will keep moisture out of the muzzle on very wet days.

Slings

Slings help the hunter carry his firearm over long distances. Custom swivels for slings are available for blackpowder guns. Also available are detachable slings that slip over the stock and barrel. Slip-on slings often have a boot that slips over the butt and a slit cut in the tip of the strap. The slip-knot formed when the strap is pulled through the slit fits over the muzzle end of the barrel and the boot holds it to the butt. Your gun's weight keeps the sling on. More modern slings made of nylon with built-in slip knots are also common.

Photos by Mike Strandlund

A gun case helps protect a gun's finish from abrasions and moisture. It also adds a margin of safety during transport.

Gun Cases

Carrying cases protect your blackpowder gun from scratches and damage. Blackpowder supply houses carry a selection of these in a variety of lengths. In the field, particularly on horseback, a scabbard will guard your gun from weather damage and make it easier to carry. A selection of camouflage covers is also available to conceal glare and help you blend into your surroundings during still-hunting, stalking, or stand hunting.

Slings, either traditional leather or modern nylon, make toting a rifle easier and in some cases safer.

Speed Loaders

A speed loader is an accessory that holds all load components at the ready, with premeasured powder and with components in convenient positions for quick loading. Speed loaders cut reloading time and are used by many hunters in place of separately carried load components.

53

Photo by Mike Strandlund

Photo by Rick Hacker

Many hunters carry speedloaders for a quicker follow-up shot and to keep load components organized and accessible.

There are a couple different types of speed loaders. The most commonly used is a commercial model consisting of a capped plastic tube. To use the speed loader, the hinged top is opened, and a premeasured powder charge is emptied into the barrel. The other end of the tube, containing a patched ball or prelubricated conical, is placed over the muzzle and a short starter pushes the bullet out of the tube and into the bore. After the bullet is seated, a percussion cap, contained in a small pocket in the tube cap, is set on the nipple.

The loading block is a more primitive type of speed loader. It is a simple block of wood with prelubricated, patched balls placed into bullet-sized holes. This block is usually carried around the neck on a leather thong or in the shooting bag. When a second shot is needed, a measure of powder is poured from an individual-charge container—often a capped plastic vial. The long arm of the short starter is used to push the prepatched ball from the block into the muzzle of the barrel. Some muzzleloader hunters use homemade speedloaders made of wood, cardboard or plastic. You can put together your own speed loaders using waterproof plastic containers, or bag them ready-made.

Shooting Bags

The muzzleloader hunter must have a container to carry his

Photo by Rick Hacker

A shooting bag is almost mandatory for the black-powder hunter to carry all the necessary shooting supplies afield.

array of shooting accessories in the woods. These shooting or "possibles" bags should be chosen with practicality in mind. Like the powderhorn, they can get in the way if they don't fit properly; they can get caught on a branch and the contents can fall out. A shooting bag can be as simple or as elaborate as you like; one with separate compartments is the most easy to keep organized. A good substitute is the modern fanny pack.

Safety Devices

Very few muzzleloaders come with a mechanical safety. The half-cock notch will stop the hammer but is not a safety. If the hammer should catch in brush when you're in the woods, then snap forward, it could cause an accidental discharge.

A piece of surgical tubing, cut to fit over the nipple, can act as a safety device for caplocks. So can an add-on pencil eraser or commercial nipple-sealing device. A flat piece of rubber or leather can also be placed between the hammer and cap. For flintlocks, a frizzen boot, made of soft leather and fit to cover the face of the frizzen, performs the same function. If the cock falls, the flint grabs the leather and jams against the face of the frizzen to keep a gun from firing. Both types of safety can be attached to the trigger guard with a small string.

Maintenance Supplies

Ramrod Attachments

There are several accessories that attach to the end of the ramrod designed for cleaning, loading, or both.

The cleaning jag screws to the tip of the rod and must fit the width of the bore and the shape of the breech. If not, it can stick so badly that the gun's breech may have to be removed to reach the jag. The cleaning patch fits over the end of the jag, and thus the entire inside surface of the bore and breech can be cleaned. The jag is equipped with grooves to hold onto the patch during the cleaning and withdrawing process.

The bore brush and breech scraper also facilitate removal of fouling. The brush must fit snugly so it will scrub the bottom and corners of the grooves. Breech scrapers, made in a variety

Photo by Mike Strandlund

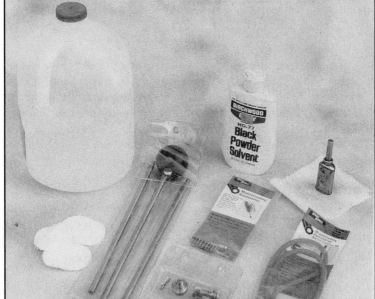

Gun maintenance is a major concern of the muzzleloader hunter. Some supplies that should be kept on hand include workrod and tips, patches, solvent, oil, flushing hose, and a jug of detergent and water.

of configurations, remove fouling from the very back of the breech (the face of a breech plug). A breech scraper resembles a flat screwdriver blade slightly smaller than the size of the bore. Some late-model caplock rifles have patent breeches with a small chamber in the face of the breech. The breech scraper must be specially designed to reach this area.

The cleaning worm is a hooked, coiled ramrod attachment for pulling out a stuck cleaning patch.

Solvents

Some of the lubricants used in loading will also function as fouling remover if they are in liquid form. This includes water soluble oil, often referred to as moose milk. A mixture of five parts alcohol and one part hydrogen peroxide is an effective and readily available solvent. So is the ether-based engine starter available in automotive stores. A thorough cleaning after hunting is essential, and a lubricant applied after cleaning will help prevent rust. It's a good idea to pull the lock and clean out the residue periodically to insure good operation. Make sure the solvent is removed before loading.

Miscellaneous Cleaning Supplies

During the cleaning process it is a good idea to check the sights on your blackpowder gun. Some tape or Loc-tite on screw-adjustable sights prevents them from slipping. A metal-bristled brush is also handy for reaching into lock crevices and other out-of-the-way places during cleaning.

Pipecleaners are helpful for cleaning the flash channel and hard-to-clean places in the lock of your gun.

Clothing

Clothing for the muzzleloading hunter should be functional but otherwise is a matter of personal preference. Part of the fun of blackpowder hunting is combining the traditional with the modern. Some hunters carry this concept into selection of their clothing. The blackpowder hunters of 200 years ago had the best equipment they could buy or barter. The blackpowder hunter of today should follow that tradition.

The basic principles in dressing for hunting are to choose clothes that keep you safe and comfortable, and that enhance your chance for success.

Photo by Mike Strandlund   *Photo by Tom Fegely*

Muzzleloader hunting seasons can occur during the heat of late summer or cold of midwinter. You may be concerned mainly with camouflaging yourself from the animal or being visible to other hunters. These and several other factors will govern how you choose your hunting wardrobe.

Outerwear and Underwear

Like any category of clothing, outerwear comes in a variety of styles with different purposes. The most important considerations are visibility, insulation, water repellency, and quietness.

Because of its high visibility, blaze orange clothing reduces hunting accidents. Check your state hunting regulations for any blaze orange requirements. During the regular gun hunting season for big game, most states require a minimum of 100 square inches (about the equivalent of a hat) of blaze orange material visible above the waist. Some states require more; some require it for small game hunting.

Camouflage clothing, on the other hand, makes you hard to see by animals, allowing you to get closer for a better shot. There are many patterns of camouflage available, from tree bark to winter woods to dead grass, along with the traditional green and brown woodland patterns. In addition a camouflage blaze orange is available; it is often a good compromise between safety and concealment. Check your regulations, because some states do not consider camouflage patterns on blaze orange sufficiently safe.

The design and heaviness of the coat you choose will depend on the season and the weather. For early season, a hooded sweatshirt may be more than warm enough. For late seasons in the

Photos by Mike Strandlund

Hunting clothes should be functional. This hunter has chosen insulated coveralls for warmth in early winter. His clothing is mainly camouflaged to avoid detection by deer, but his blaze orange cap provides safety.

For optimum comfort while hunting, dress in layers. The innermost layer should be polypropylene or a similar fabric that wicks moisture from the skin. Middle layers should provide insulation, while the outer layer should repel water and provide camouflage or visibility.

north, you may need a heavy winter coat with down or high-quality synthetic insulation. Most hunters need to adapt their clothing throughout the day to changes in weather and exertion. It is best in these cases to dress in layers, so that clothing can be added and removed for optimum comfort.

Rain gear is important to have handy in most parts of the country. Select rain gear that either makes you more visible or less visible, whichever is appropriate. A most useful modern item for the blackpowder hunter gear is an ordinary poncho. It can provide excellent protection from wet weather for both the hunter and his muzzleloader, and it can provide better concealment or visibility than regular clothes, depending upon color. It can be easily stashed away when no longer needed and can double as ground cover or back pad.

One of the main drawbacks of wearing rain gear is the noise it makes when you touch brush or even move a little bit. Some other outerwear is made with an outer shell of synthetic fabric with similar noisy qualities. This is a major detriment to most types of hunting, and the hunter should choose clothing that is quiet. Wool, cotton, and some new quiet synthetics are among the best.

Cotton is not a good choice for underwear because it absorbs moisture and stays wet. Wool keeps you warm even when wet, but can cause itching. Polypropylene and other synthetic fabrics that "wick" moisture from the skin into the outer layers of clothes are best for underwear.

Footwear
Footwear is a vital part of any hunter's wardrobe. You must choose the correct style and fit—footwear with tread and protection appropriate for the terrain, temperature, and dampness. For rocky terrain, soft soles and deep treads are best, while hard soles are hard to beat for traction in sand or mud. Deep-track soles become caked with mud, losing traction and gaining weight. All-rubber boots are best for hunters who want to keep the water out and their scent in. Pacs and "bunny boots" are the warmest; nylon hiking shoes are the most comfortable in warm weather.

Clothing Accessories
The type of clothing accessories you choose depends on several factors. Wear the proper hat for the climate. Select a cap with a visor for good protection against glare, or ear protectors for warmth. A wide-brimmed hat offers good rain protection. Hoods on jackets offer the best warmth but can impair your hearing.

Gloves not only keep your hands warm, but can help hide the conspicuous visual alarm created by moving, light-colored hands. Some hunters can shoot while wearing a light pair of gloves. In colder weather, mittens you can remove quickly in a shooting situation or with a finger opening are usually best.

NRA Staff Photos

Hunting boots provide varying degrees of warmth, traction, and water repellency. Selecting the proper footwear is crucial to comfort on a hunt.

Hunting Aids

A variety of hunting equipment will make life easier in the field when you hunt with black powder.

Optics

Binoculars may not be traditional muzzleloader hunting gear, although "spy glasses" were often used by pioneer buckskinners. Anyone who has taken binoculars hunting is reluctant to hunt without them. They are a tremendous aid for the hunter in finding game and counting points. You may be able to spot an animal from long distance and make a stalk. Or you can carefully scan an area for game without having to walk it, saving time.

The quality of binoculars varies considerably; try before you buy. Seven or eight power binoculars are usually best. Unless they are high quality, high-magnification binoculars can be more of a liability than an asset. Eyepiece shields guard against moisture and glare.

Compact binoculars, which weigh as little as eight ounces, are often ideal for the hunter. Larger models offering a higher magnification, field of view, and variable power in some cases, may be an advantage.

Spotting scopes provide much higher magnification than binoculars and are useful for systematic scoping in open country.

Shooting and safety glasses are other optical equipment the hunter should consider. Yellow or amber eyeglass lenses improve

Photo by Mike Strandlund

Binoculars are a very valuable hunting aid, allowing you to search for game from afar and judge animals closely.

contrast in low-light conditions experienced during sunrise and sunset, and are the optimum in shooting glasses for the blackpowder hunter. Shooting glasses further protect your eyes from flying debris when shooting a muzzleloader. The only drawback is that the lenses may reflect light and alert an animal, but this can be offset by the shade of a large- brimmed hat, and the safety advantages outweigh any disadvantage.

Calls, Scents, and Decoys

Depending on the kind of animal you hunt, you may want to try to bring the game to you by using a call, an attractive scent, or decoys.

Nearly any type of game can be called or lured to the hunter, and manufacture of the products used in these techniques has become big business. Big birds are the most commonly attracted types of game, through the use of calls and decoys. Hunters use both calls and decoys for waterfowl and turkeys. Elk and moose hunters have used mating calls to attract those animals for centuries. More recently, deer calling and rattling have become popular among hunters, and food and sex scents are also in widespread use. Hunters of predators, other types of big game, and even small game use calls today.

Techniques that involve attracting game to you are more complex and require more knowledge than most other types of hunting. These methods can be quite costly, especially if you decoy waterfowl or use a lot of special animal scents.

Photo by Mike Strandlund

Commercial tree stands have become very popular, especially among whitetail hunters. They provide an elevated position that helps you avoid the animal's eyes and nose, yet are portable for fast and easy relocation.

Portable Tree Stands

The muzzleloader hunter seeking big game must get as close to the game as possible to set up the shot. One of the best ways of getting a close shot is with a tree stand. Tree stands put you out of the game's line of view in many cases, and also help disperse your scent.

You can build your own tree stand or just sit in a large-branched tree, but the use of portable tree stands is becoming the most popular among muzzleloader hunters.

There are many different designs of portables. Some you chain to a tree, others you actually use to climb the tree, and others have attached ladders. There are several tree stand accessories available, including safety harnesses and screw-in or strap-on steps.

Woodsmanship and Travel Gear

Next in importance after clothing, gun, and ammo are the items that keep you safe and in control outdoors.

First, you need a way to carry your gear. You may be able to get it into big pockets, but a pack is preferable.

For a small amount of gear, a fanny pack may be best. It rides around your hips and does not restrict shoulder movement. For more gear, a small backpack is necessary.

Don't buy a cheap pack; get a heavy duty bag with tough zippers. A few manufacturers make packs of tough cotton, which is very quiet in the woods. Nylon is more durable and sheds water easily.

Camping Equipment

On an extended hunting trip, you'll need camping equipment. This is an important matter, one that you must carefully consider. The easiest way to camp is with a camp trailer or pickup camper. Your temporary home is self-contained, and you won't need to worry much about weather. A motorhome is questionable, unless you address two important items. First, you must never drive it off secondary roads because of the possibility of getting it stuck. This requirement precludes the possibility of getting in close to good game country. Second, you should tow a hunting vehicle with your motorhome, or you won't be mobile. It's vital to have a dependable means of transportation.

Tenting is popular among hunters on several-day trips. Though a tent doesn't offer all the services that a hard-sided unit does, it takes up little space and can be erected almost anywhere. Various heat systems keep tent interiors warm.

Tents come in a variety of designs, each for a different purpose. Most popular today is the three-man dome tent with a removable rain fly. It is a good compromise in weight, price, and roominess. For long stays, you'll appreciate the extra space provided by a larger dome tent or wall tent.

Very small tents are seldom worth buying, with one exception. There are high-quality, one-man tents available that weigh only a couple pounds and can be carried routinely in a daypack. In a survival situation, or if you spot game in evening far from main camp and want to be there at first light, you can simply pull out your tent and set up a comfortable spike camp.

Your tent must be waterproof. It's a good idea to test the tent before your comfort or even survival depends on it. Erect the tent and set a lawn sprinkler so it thoroughly sprays the tent for several hours.

Canvas tents are still popular, but most of them leak where you touch them. For extra protection, apply a layer of plastic over the roof and secure it tightly so the wind doesn't tear it off.
Your tent should have a floor. If not, use a tarp or piece of plastic. Either could get damp, but at least you'll be free of dirt.

Photo by Jim Hower

On an extended hunt, a comfortable, well-provisioned camp is important.

Some campers spread straw, leaves, or pine needles on the ground when using a floorless tent.

Sleeping cots will provide much more comfort than sleeping on an air mattress or directly on the ground. Air mattresses sometimes leak, and they're so small you often roll off during the night. A cot has a small amount of sag and tends to hold you securely. Be sure you put a foam pad on the cot. It provides more cushion and also keeps you a great deal warmer. Your sleeping bag will compress below you, providing no loft, and you'll be cold and miserable, even in a quality bag if you lie on a cot without a pad.

If you're camping in cold country, a heater will be a nice addition. You can use a wood stove that is collapsible and is transported easily, or you can fire up a kerosene stove. The latter will take the chill out of your tent, but if it's really cold, the wood stove is tops for yielding maximum heat. Catalytic heaters are widely used, but they're not effective if it's windy and bitterly cold. Whatever method of heating you use, be sure there's adequate ventilation to avoid asphyxiation.

Firewood will be necessary if you heat with a wood stove. Bring along sharp tools. A small chain saw saves time, and be aware of regulations regarding firewood cutting. A permit from the land agency might be required.

Some kind of lighting around camp is required. Flashlights are fine for small chores, but you should have a central unit that provides good illumination. Lanterns are standard, and are fueled by a disposable propane tank or white gas. Be sure you have more fuel than you think you'll need, and bring along a supply of mantles. Wooden matches are best to light the mantles because the flame source must be pushed up through a slot, and larger matches work best.

Sleeping Gear

If you hunt out of a lodge, motel, or boarding house, you might have the luxury of sheets and blankets. It's more likely, however, that you'll be spending your nights in a sleeping bag.

Down bags are expensive and will keep you warm during very cold temperatures. Be aware, however, that there are various grades of down. Some sleeping bags are filled with duck feathers or have only a certain percentage of down. Goose down is the premier filler, and is the most expensive. The label on the bag should identify the kind of down and how many ounces are in the bag.

For all its warmth, down is worthless if it gets wet. The bag will be clammy and cold, and it will take forever to dry.

Synthetic fillers, on the other hand, are easily dried and will retain heat even when wet because they retain their loft. Most are not as expensive as down, but some will keep you just as warm. When shopping for sleeping bags, check their ratings. Some will keep you warm at 15 degrees, some at zero, and some even lower. The amount of loft is a good indicator of the bag's quality. More loft means more heat retention capabilities. The warmth of whatever sleeping bag you have can be increased considerably with a heat-conserving liner.

When packing your sleeping bag, make sure it's in a waterproof container if you're packing in on a horse. It could get wet during the packing operation or on the ride in. An easy way to protect the bag is to simply seal it tightly in two or three heavy-duty garbage bags.

Emergency Kit

This kit should always be included on a hunting trip. It should be small enough to carry with you, and large enough to accommodate the following:

- **Space Blanket for protection against cold and wet**
- **Waterproof container of matches**
- **Paraffin-coated kindling**
- **Dehydrated or dried high-energy foods**
- **Miscellaneous first-aid items (especially burn medication and eye wash or drops)**
- **Backup compass and knife**
- **Signal mirror and whistle to help others locate you**
- **Spare prescription medicines and eyeglasses, if applicable**

Depending on the circumstances, you may add some items such as extra water, a snake-bite kit, or warm clothes.

Field Dressing Gear

If you are big game hunting on foot, take an extra pack frame or two to help carry out your game meat and trophy. In addition, include the following butchering and field dressing tools:

- **Dressing/skinning knife (perhaps with gut hook)**
- **Fillet knife**
- **Small block and tackle**
- **Nylon cord**
- **Meat bags or cheesecloth for covering the meat**
- **Tape measure (for measuring a trophy for taxidermy purposes)**
- **Small folding saw or hatchet for separating bone**

Compass

This is an item of equipment that should be carried by every hunter. Don't bother with cheap compasses; they can cause more trouble than they save. Get a high-quality model with luminescent dial. Know how to use it.

Compasses come in a variety of designs, including those you carry in your pocket, pin to your coat, and strap on your wrist. The best models are those with adjustable direction-bearing dials and a strong cord to secure it to yourself.

Photo by Mike Strandlund

Among the most important gear for a hunter in strange territory is a map and compass. Used correctly, they keep you from getting lost, make travel easier, and help you find game.

Knives

As with any type of hunting gun or gear, knives come in an array of shapes and sizes, and you have to decide which best suits your needs. The main function of a hunting knife is to field dress the animal. A light knife with a three- or four-inch blade is ample, and even a two-inch penknife could do the job. There are specialized knives designed for gutting game, with a hook or blade protector that make splitting the belly as easy as undoing a zipper.

A small knife usually serves the hunter best because it is light and unobtrusive. Large sheath knives are heavy, get caught on brush, and may poke you in the kidney when you sit down. They are unwieldy in precise jobs. On the other hand, a large knife may be more practical if you foresee heavy-duty jobs like splitting a pelvic bone, cutting poles, or performing other heavy duties.

Photo by Joe Workosky

On extended hunts, it is best to have a small knife for smaller jobs and a big blade for big ones. Be sure to bring a sharpening stone.

Equipment Considerations

Go over your gear list carefully before you leave home. The biggest mistake is packing too much rather than not enough. Just remember the words *cold* and *wet*. Prepare for both and you'll be in good shape.

Following is a basic list to get you started:

- **Gun**
- **Ammo, Powder, and Shooting Supplies**
- **Knife**
- **Compass and Maps**
- **Binoculars and other Optics**
- **Decoys, Calls, or Scents**
- **Toilet Paper**
- **Sleeping Bag, Pad, and Pillow**
- **Flashlight or Lantern**
- **Extra Batteries and Fuel**
- **Tent, Stakes**
- **Small Tool Kit**
- **Camp Stove**
- **Camp Stool**
- **Emergency Kit**
- **Fire-Building Materials**
- **Heater, Fuel**
- **Prescription Medications**
- **Water**
- **Water Purification Tablets**
- **Spare Clothing (Especially Gloves, Socks, Hat, Boots, Sweater)**
- **Food and Drink**
- **Rope**
- **Saw or Axe**
- **Shovel**
- **Spare Eyeglasses**
- **Cooking and Eating Utensils**
- **Shave Kit, Wash Cloth, Towel**
- **Camera and Film**
- **Cooler**
- **Plastic Bags**
- **Snowshoes or Skis**
- **Horsemanship Gear**

Part II
Muzzleloader Shooting for Hunters

Photo by Tom Fegely

CHAPTER 4

LOADING, SHOOTING AND MAINTAINING THE MUZZLELOADER

While many blackpowder firearms hobbyists own and shoot muzzleloaders because they enjoy tinkering with the gun, many hunters tend to consider operation of the gun secondary to the hunt. But when it comes to loading, shooting, and maintaining the muzzleloader, you must momentarily put aside excitement of the chase and concentrate on the gun. For safety, good operation, and preservation of the firearm, total attention must be given to loading and maintaining the muzzleloader.

Photo by Mike Strandlund

Before hunting, a muzzleloader shooter must thoroughly familiarize himself with loading, shooting, and maintaining his gun.

Loading

As the name suggests, a muzzleloader is loaded by inserting load components into the bore by way of the muzzle. This necessitates that the shooter's fingers are directly in front of the muzzle during most of the loading process. It doesn't take much imagination to realize what could happen if the gun should accidentally discharge during loading or cleaning. This and other conditions require that safety be the dominant consideration during loading, cleaning, and all other handling of the muzzleloader.

Photo by Mike Strandlund

Prior to loading, always make sure your gun's breech and bore are clean and clear. With a percussion gun, the final step in this procedure is to snap a cap, watching to make sure air is expelled from the muzzle.

Always consult your gun manual for information on these procedures. If you do not have a manual, the manufacturer will probably provide one for free.

Loading Blackpowder Rifles

Following are the steps in loading a muzzleloading rifle:

Step 1 – Position the rifle for loading. Place the butt of the gun on the ground with the muzzle facing away from your face. Hold the rifle between your legs, if you can do so with good stability, or else hold it alongside your body.

Step 2 – Check whether the rifle is already loaded. With the muzzle pointed in a safe direction, insert the ramrod to the bottom of the barrel. Mark the ramrod at the muzzle, remove it, and hold the ramrod against the outside of the barrel. If the length of the ramrod that fits in the barrel will extend from the muzzle to the nipple or flash channel, the rifle is unloaded. If the rifle is loaded, it should be cleared by pulling the bullet—the procedure is described later in this chapter. Clear the load by firing it only if you put it there and know it is a safe charge.

Step 3 – Wipe out the bore and flash channel. If stored properly, the inside of the rifle will be coated with oil. This must be removed

Charging a Muzzleloading Rifle

(A) Use a mark on your ramrod to make sure the rifle is not loaded.
(B) Wipe the bore free of oil.
(C) Measure the powder charge and pour it through the muzzle.

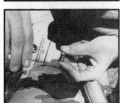

(D) Lubricate the patch or bullet.
(E) Start the bullet into the muzzle with the short starter.
(F) If using bulk patching material, trim the patch.

(G) Seat the bullet firmly on the powder charge
(H) Prime the pan or set the cap. Put the gun into a safe condition until ready to shoot.

Photos by Mike Strandlund

to prevent oil from soaking into the black powder or blocking the flash channel. Swab the bore with dry patches, being sure to swab the bottom of the breech. Wipe out the flash channel by removing the nipple or clean-out screw and swabbing the channel with pipecleaners. On percussion guns snap a cap or two with the muzzle pointed close to loose ground litter; if the channel is clear, the concussion will visibly disturb a leaf or blade of grass. With a flintlock, wipe the pan with a dry cloth, or ignite a light priming charge at the flash hole, then clear the channel of soot with a flash hole pick. Before proceeding, set the gun's hammer on half-cock.

Step 4 – Prepare the powder charge. Use reliable loading information and a black powder measure. Select the correct powder granulation and use a fairly light load for initial test firing.

Step 5 – Charge the barrel. Pour the powder into the measure from its container, far from any source of high heat, and immediately close the powder container. With the rifle standing barrel-up with the muzzle angled away from you, pour the powder down the barrel. Tap the barrel with your hand to free any powder that may be clinging to the bore and to ensure powder enters the flash channel.

Step 6 – Prepare the projectile for loading. With conical bullets, you must first coat the bullet with a lubricant. The hollow bases of minie bullets may be filled with grease, while solid maxi bullet

Photos by Mike Strandlund

To load a rifle with a commercial speedloader, pop the top and dump the premeasured powder charge down the bore. Set the narrow end of the tube over the muzzle, and ram the bullet. Press the cap onto the nipple.

bases should be free of lubricant. The conical is then started into the bore with thumb pressure, with care that the bullet goes in straight. To prepare round balls, first lubricate patching material or use a pretrimmed, prelubricated patch. Set the patch on the muzzle, with the ball on top. With cast balls, the sprue must point up, out of the barrel.

Step 7 – Short-start the projectile. The bullet is rammed the first few inches with a short-starter. Insert the bullet just inside the muzzle with the shortest shaft. If you're using a round ball and large patching material, this is the point where any excess patching material is trimmed off flush with the muzzle. Use the longer shaft of the short-starter to ram the bullet another few inches.

Step 8 – Seat the projectile. Use the ramrod to move the bullet down the bore to the powder. Grasp the ramrod close to the muzzle, and move the bullet down the bore a few inches at a time with short, firm strokes, until you feel it seat against the powder. Seat the bullet firmly against the powder charge using firm, even pressure of about 30 to 50 pounds. Use the same pressure each time for optimum accuracy. Use a muzzle protector if you are using a steel workrod.

At this point it is wise for the beginner to test the load to be sure it is seated. Toss a wooden ramrod against the load a couple times. If it stops dead against the ball, the load is not seated. If it bounces back up the bore, the load is correctly in place. You may use this procedure to seat your first load, then mark the ramrod at the point where it leaves the muzzle. This will serve as reference for knowing when future loads are seated. Don't use this method where accuracy is important, because the procedure will deform the projectile. Keep in mind that if fouling accumulates at the back of the breech, you will not be able to seat the load as far down the bore. The ramrod may extend a quarter-inch farther out of a dirty bore. Keep the breech free of fouling with a breech scraper.

Step 9 – Prime the gun. When you're ready to shoot the gun or go hunting, you may set the cap on the nipple of percussion rifles or prime the pan of flintlocks. On caplocks, simply cock the hammer and slip the cap over the nipple, being very careful to keep the muzzle pointed in a safe direction and your fingers away from the trigger. Press the cap firmly but not hard. On flintlocks, put a pinch of FFFFg powder in the pan so powder fills the pan up to (but not into) the flash channel. Keep the cock on half-cock until ready to shoot.

Loading Blackpowder Shotguns

Steps 1, 2, 3 – Position, check, and clean. Before loading a muzzleloading shotgun, position it, check to see if it is loaded, and wipe it out as described for rifles. Set hammers of percussion guns on half-cock.

Charging a Muzzleloading Shotgun

Photos by Mike Strandlund

(A) Wipe the bores free of oil.
(B) Measure powder charges and pour through the muzzles.

If the shotgun is a double-barrel, you must develop a foolproof system of loading so you do not get confused and load double charges in one barrel, or get the components mixed up. It's safest to cover one barrel while you load the other completely; then cover the charged barrel as you load the empty one. Some shooters place the ramrod in the empty barrel as they load each component in the other. Always start with the same barrel to avoid confusion. Double-charging a barrel can be disastrous.

Step 4 – Measure the black powder. Use a relatively light powder charge initially.

Step 5 – Charge the barrel with powder.

Step 6 – Place the wad column. Insert the over-powder buffer — just a wad or a card and wad. The thin card wad is angled slightly as it is placed into the tube to get it past a choke constriction. It will straighten as you push it down the bore with the large-ended shotgun ramrod. Set the card firmly against the powder, holding it there for a moment to let any compressed air escape. (If you don't hold each card or wad in place at each step, compressed air may push the card upward, creating a gap between powder and wad that could make the barrel explode.) If you feel air pressure force the wad up as you let up on the ramrod, press it back down until it stays.

Insert the fiber cushion wad and/or shot cup. A fiber wad may be dampened (not saturated) with lubricant before it is inserted, but lubrication may not be necessary. Slide it down the bore and seat it firmly on the over-powder card.

Photos by Mike Strandlund

(C) Insert over-powder wads.
(D) Measure shot and pour through the muzzles.

(E) Insert over-shot cards or wads.
(F) Set the caps and put the gun into a safe condition until ready to shoot.

Step 7 – Load the shot. Measure a shot charge with a dipper or calibrated volume measure, and pour it down the barrel.

Step 8 – Place the over-shot card or wad. Set either a thin card or thick wad (cards are usually preferred) in the muzzle and ram it down the bore to the shot. Seat firmly, but not so hard that the pellets may be deformed. Be sure this card is unlubricated, to help insure it won't slip under weight of the shot charge.

Step 9 – Repeat for second barrel.

Step 10 – Prime the gun when ready to shoot or beginning to hunt. When shooting a particular load, you may mark the ramrod to tell you at what depth it is properly seated. It is best to use a pencil or tape to mark the ramrod if you plan on using various types of loads, which will take up varying amounts of space in the barrel.

If you shoot only one barrel of a double-barrel, deprime and check the unfired tube to see if the load is still well seated. Sometimes recoil from one barrel may dislodge the load in the other. The loose load will shoot a poor pattern and may be a safety hazard.

Loading Blackpowder Pistols

A single-shot muzzleloading pistol is loaded the same way you load a rifle, with extra care because muzzle control is more difficult with shorter-barreled guns. Revolvers require a different procedure for loading, as follows:

Step 1 – Be sure the gun is unloaded. Check each chamber in the cylinder to make sure the revolver is unloaded and uncapped, and that there is no foreign matter in the chambers. Set the hammer at half-cock so the cylinder will rotate freely.

Step 2 – Clean the bore and chambers. Wipe the gun free of excess oil and snap a cap or two on each of the chambers.

Step 3 – Position the pistol for loading. Hold it either in a loading rack or between your knees as you kneel, with the muzzle pointed away from your face.

Charging a Cap and Ball Revolver

Photos by Rick Hacker

(A) Wipe cylinders free of oil.
   (B) Measure and pour powder into the first cylinder.

Step 4 – Measure the charge. Set your powder measure for the correct charge and fill with powder.

Step 5 – Load each chamber with powder. If you're planning to carry the revolver in the field, load only five chambers, resting the hammer over the empty chamber.

Step 6 – Load the projectiles. Set a ball in the first chamber, position the ball under the loading lever, and seat the ball firmly into the chamber with the lever. Because no patch is used, the lead ball must be a bit larger in circumference than the chamber

Photos by Rick Hacker

(C) Place ball over mouth of cylinder, on top of patch if you wish to use one.
   (D) Ram the ball into the cylinder, and repeat these four steps for five of the six cylinders.

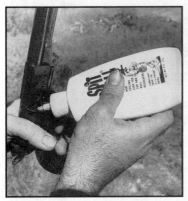

(E) Fill cylinder mouths with grease to prevent chain-firing.
   (F) Cap the nipples after five cylinders have been loaded, and rest the hammer on the empty chamber until ready for firing.

81

mouth. To check this, make sure a small ring of lead is shaved off the ball at each chamber mouth.

Step 7 – Seal the chambers. With the imperfect fit of the bare lead ball in each chamber, it is possible that sparks from a shot could ignite the powder in a nearby chamber. To prevent this chain-firing, the mouths of the chambers are filled with heavy grease, which is struck level with the front of the cylinder.

The grease also helps lubricate the bore of the revolver, and keeps the fouling soft and easier to remove. Grease is messy, however, especially when the revolver is carried by the hunter throughout a warm day. An alternative way to avoid dangerous and damaging multiple discharges is to use an over-powder wad. Immediately after all chambers have been charged with powder, a wad of the right proportions is inserted and set snugly on the powder with the loading lever, followed by the ball. Another method is to use corn meal over the powder before seating the ball.

Step 8 – Prime the gun when ready to shoot or beginning to hunt.

NRA Staff Photo

A properly fitting ball will leave a bit of shaved lead at the cylinder mouth of a revolver after it is rammed.

Shooting the Hunting Muzzleloader

The fundamentals of all rifle, shotgun, and pistol shooting apply to muzzleloaders. There are also special considerations.

The first step in shooting is to determine from which side of your body to shoot the gun. This is not dependent on whether you are right- or left-handed, but whether your right eye or left eye is dominant.

Photo by Mike Strandlund

The first step in learning to shoot is to determine which of your eyes is dominant. Shoot from the shoulder that is on the same side of your body as your dominant eye.

To determine eye dominance, focus with both eyes on a small, distant object. Hold your hands at arm's length, palms outward, and frame the object in a small opening between your hands. Slowly draw your hands back toward your face, keeping both eyes open. You will find that your hands are drawn to one eye—that is your dominant eye.

If you find your right eye is dominant, you should shoot a gun from your right side, even if you are left-handed. There are few exceptions. Some shooters do not have a dominant eye; both are equal. A few shooters have an overriding reason to shoot from the side opposite their dominant eye. In these cases, shooters should close their eye that is farthest from the gun. The majority of shooters have best results shooting any type of sporting arm with both eyes open.

83

Rifle Shooting

The correct hold is fundamental to accurate shooting with the hunting muzzleloader. Grasping the fore-end lightly and the grip firmly, snug the buttstock of the rifle into the pocket of your shoulder—below the collarbone between the pectoral muscle and the shoulder joint. The proper hold on a rifle that fits you should put the sights nearly on alignment when you shoulder the gun. Depending on the drop at comb—the difference between the plane of the barrel and the plane of the buttstock—you may have to adjust the hold of your trigger hand. With a straight-stocked rifle, a shooter may have to roll his trigger hand down a bit to keep his thumb from interfering with his view of the sights.

Photo by Gerald Almy

A well-fitting gun and proper hold is necessary to reach your potential in accuracy with a muzzleloader.

The standard shooting position for sighting-in and target shooting is the bench rest, described in Chapter 5. It is the steadiest position, but obviously impossible for a hunting situation. A close approximation in a hunting situation is to use crossed sticks. The other positions have varying steadiness—the hunter should always strive for the steadiest position to make the shot.

Most hunters have the best accuracy while lying on their belly with a solid rest, but this is difficult to do with the stock design of some muzzleloaders. The next steadiest rest, and usually more comfortable and practical, is seated with a solid rest. Standing with a rest is somewhat steadier than the semisupported seated position, in which the hunter sits with his ankles crossed, left over right (for a right-handed hunter) with his elbows supported on the insides of his knees. It is more solid than a kneeling position, and much better than the standing offhand position, which is seldom a practical position for the hunter. A rifleman should almost always be able to find a steadier position than offhand when shooting at game.

Many rifle hunters hunt from blinds, posts, or tree stands, and can utilize these positions for a solid rest. Blinds should have a solid rifle rest built in. Hunters can also build rifle rests into permanent tree stands and position themselves in portable stands for at least a semisupported sitting position.

Along with shooting position, the sight picture, breath control, trigger squeeze, and follow-through are also important in rifle-shooting accuracy. In most hunting situations the most accurate sighting method with iron sights is to isolate a very small spot on the center of the target animal's heart/lung vital zone. Align the front sight so the center of the tip just covers that spot, with the front sight centered and even with the top of the rear sight. Sighting is similar with an aperture sight, only the front sight is centered in the round opening of the rear sight. If your marksmanship is good enough to allow you to shoot to long distances, your sight picture will have to change accordingly to compensate for bullet trajectory (this is detailed in Chapter 5).

As you fire the shot, you must steady the sights, hold your breath, squeeze the trigger, and follow through. Take a couple of deep breaths, stop breathing, and concentrate on holding.

Align the sights on the small spot on the target and keep them as close to that small spot as possible. The front sight will move some; as it passes over your target spot, put slight pressure on the trigger until the sight moves away. Hold the pressure, then apply more as the sight passes over the spot again. Discharging the rifle should not be a conscious act; yet it should not take you completely by surprise. Each time the sight passes over the target spot and you apply pressure, you know the gun could discharge, but you do not discharge it deliberately.

The entire process should take no more than eight or 10 seconds. If you have difficulty holding your breath this long, relax, take a deep breath, and begin again if the shooting situation will allow.

Photo by Mike Strandlund

The keys to rifle marksmanship are a steady rest, proper breath control, smooth trigger squeeze, and steady follow-through.

As the rifle discharges, you must maintain your hold as long as possible for optimum accuracy. This is called follow-through, and is most important with muzzleloaders—especially flintlocks, which may have a noticeable lapse of time before complete discharge. Failure to follow-through leads to flinching, which pulls the sights off target. With proper follow-through, consciousness of your hold should remain through discharge, so that you are aware of where the sights were when the gun fired. You should be able to "call the shot," or know about where the bullet hit.

Shotgun Shooting

While rifle shooting primarily involves steadiness and control, accuracy with shotgun shooting involves more reflexes and timing.

The fundamentals of eye dominance, hold, and stance are important when developing shotgun skills. The shooter holds the shotgun on the side of his dominant eye, with his opposite foot slightly ahead of the other in the direction of the target. The shotgun should fit so that when the shooter raises it to his shoulder, he is naturally looking down the barrel with the thumb of his trigger hand about an inch from his nose.

There are three basic ways of shooting airborne targets with a shotgun. The swing-through method consists of the gunner swinging the muzzle of the shotgun faster than the target is moving; the bead comes up from behind and past the target, and the shooter times his trigger pull to coincide with a certain lead. In the sustained-lead method, the shooter estimates the correct lead in front of the flying target, swings the muzzle in that area at the same speed as the target, and pulls the trigger

Photo by Mike Strandlund   *Photo by Rick Hacker*

A skillful shotgun shooter concentrates on the target even as he begins to shoulder the gun. He maintains that focus as he swings to target, shoots, and follows through.

when his lead and swing are right. The snap-shooter calculates a point in space where the shot and the target will meet, points the gun there, and pulls the trigger. Each of these methods is best in certain circumstances.

Certain fundamentals apply to all shotgunning methods. The shooter must estimate speed, lead, and muzzle swing instantly, semiconsciously. He must pull the trigger decisively, rather than squeezing it as a rifleman would. He must follow through with his swing or his point for best accuracy.

Experienced shotgunners using a muzzleloader for the first time must alter their shooting styles somewhat because of the increased time lapse between the trigger pull and the shot reaching the target. A muzzleloader, especially a flintlock, requires the shooter to lead the target more.

Pistol Shooting

The fundamentals of position, hold, breath control, trigger squeeze, and follow-through are basically the same for pistol as they are for rifle. A shooter cannot achieve as precise accuracy with a pistol as a rifle, however, because of the pistol's shorter sight radius and the difficulty in steadying the handgun.

Most pistol shooters align their sights using the "6 o'clock

NRA Staff Photo

Pistol-shooting fundamentals are similar to those for rifles, but marksmanship is more difficult to master.

hold," in which the front sight is at the bottom of the target. This method works best for shooting bullseye targets at a known distance. In close-range shooting, for which blackpowder pistols are most adapted, it is best to pick a small spot as you would with a rifle.

Pistol shooters can benefit from a solid rest even more than rifle shooters can. If you shoot without a rest, the sitting position with elbows supported inside the knees is good, as is the prone position. If you shoot offhand, use a solid two-hand grip; with a light grip, a pistol is likely to be jerked out of alignment as the trigger snaps and the hammer falls.

In target-shooting and test-firing revolvers, all chambers of the gun are loaded before shooting commences. In virtually all cases where the gun is taken hunting, it is safer and no detriment to load only five chambers of the revolver, keeping the hammer down on the empty chamber. Some percussion revolvers have safety notches between the nipples where the hammer may rest safely, but it is safer to keep the hammer on an empty chamber. There is less chance of the hammer slipping out of a notch and onto a nipple. It requires more of a conscious effort to put the hammer on an empty chamber, which keeps you concentrating on safety. Never carry a revolver fully loaded and in the half-cock position.

NRA Staff Photo

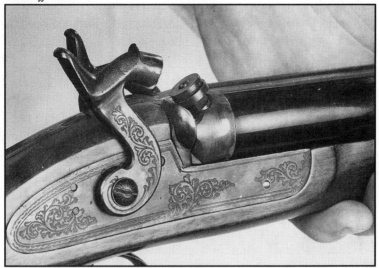

Dry-firing is a good way to practice when you can't shoot live ammo. A rubber washer or similar buffer should be used to protect a nipple from hammer blows.

Functioning Problems

The most common problem with a muzzleloader is no ignition or slow ignition. Usually it is caused by damp powder or a dirty gun. A bad cap or a dull flint can also contribute to the problem. On rare occasions, a weak spring may be at fault.

A dirty breech can be caused by improper cleaning prior to firing. Repeated firing without cleaning between shots results in debris accumulating in the breech. This "cake" builds up and eventually can block the flash channel. Prior to going hunting, clean the gun thoroughly and dry the breech.

Any moisture, even morning dew or high humidity, can render black powder useless. Extra care is required with a flintlock because the powder charge is exposed directly to the atmosphere. The priming charge will soak up moisture and become packed very easily in the early morning. Change priming regularly and clean the wet priming out by brushing it away from the flash hole. It's a good idea to open the flash hole with a pick to ensure no wet powder will block the flash.

With a caplock, misfires are caused by the cap failing to fire or by the cap failing to set off the charge. If the cap does not

Photo by Tom Fegely

Firing problems in a muzzleloader are often caused by an obstructed flash channel. Have a pick handy at all times to clear plugs.

fire, try another. If it happens again, check that the cap is the right size and that it seats well on the nipple. Check that the hammer strikes the cap squarely; if not, either the hammer or the bolster will have to be adjusted.

If the cap fires but the gun does not discharge, there is probably an obstruction in the flash channel. Some guns have unreliable ignition even with a clear flash channel, and may be helped with the installation of a high-performance nipple. Another cure is to prime the nipple—put a small pinch of fine powder just under the nipple. This often helps when the flash must make a couple of bends before reaching the main charge, but is little help with a straight flash channel such as that found on shotguns. It may also slow ignition because the powder in the drum will act like a fuse, so use this procedure only to clear a problem load.

A misfire can cause a load to become unseated. The force from the cap can cause a load to move forward, creating a danger-ous air space that could cause a breech explosion. Whenever you try the shot again following a misfire, wait at least five minutes with the muzzle in a safe direction, and reseat the projectile carefully.

A recurring misfire problem can be caused by backpressure—an air lock between the cap and powder charge resists the flash. This can be rectified by having a very small hole drilled in the bolster between the nipple and the breech to vent this backpressure. A small plug of wax or stiff grease will keep moisture from entering the vent. (Note: This should be done only by a professional gunsmith. The modification may void the warranty of some guns.)

If your rifle will not fire after repeated attempts, you must remove the charge. Work FFFFg powder through the flash hole of a flintlock with the pick and reprime and discharge into a safe backstop. Pull the nipple on a caplock and make sure it is clear. Pull the clean-out screw and make sure the channel is clear using the nipple pick to remove any debris. Try a couple more caps and discharge into a safe backstop. If the gun won't discharge, push a little FFFFg powder into the nipple channel and reinsert the nipple. Always check the bullet to make sure it is firmly down on the powder before firing.

If this approach does not work, check the ramrod mark to see if the bullet was loaded without powder. If so, or if you prefer to pull the load rather than discharge it, use a ball puller to remove the ball from the barrel. Make sure to decap or deprime prior to pulling a ball. Pour a bit of liquid lubricant or solvent

Photo by Mike Strandlund

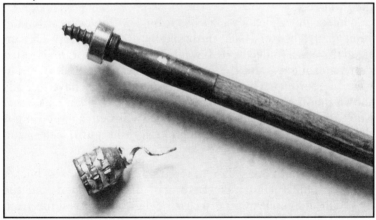

If a gun will not fire after repeated attempts, the projectile may have to be removed with a ball puller.

down the bore to dampen the patch so the ball will come out easier.

Occasionally a fouled barrel will result in a ball getting stuck halfway down the barrel. Never try to "shoot out" a bullet that is stuck part way down the barrel. It could cause the barrel to explode. Pull it, or push it down on the powder. If the ball won't move up or down, pour an ounce or two of cleaning solvent down the barrel and let it soak. Eventually it will soften the fouling and the ball can be pulled. Flush the barrel out well after this type of problem. There will be a big mess in the breech.

Occasionally caplock shooters experience blow back through the nipple when firing heavy hunting charges. This is usually caused by a worn-out nipple. Replace the nipple and problems should go away. If poor cap ignition and misfires occur in addition to blow back, the problem may be a weak lock mainspring. This problem should be corrected by a gunsmith.

Some of the more popular muzzleloaders sold today have spring-loaded adjustable sights on the barrel. A little Loc-tite applied to the screws prior to use in the field will prevent the sights from coming apart at an inopportune time.

Muzzleloader Maintenance

When a black powder gun is fired, powder fouling covers its bore, lock, and other parts. This fouling is highly corrosive because of its moisture-attracting properties. If muzzleloaders are not cleaned and oiled quickly and thoroughly after shooting, they will rust.

While a muzzleloader may be cleaned with blackpowder solvent, many shooters have traditionally used very hot water instead to clean a fouled bore. It was believed that hot water cleaned more thoroughly, and the heat quickly evaporated all traces of water. Experiments by some experts on the subject have recently shown that hot water may encourage rusting of a bore, and that water that is cool or at room temperature is better. Following is the recommended cleaning method for shotguns, rifles, and single-shot pistols:

1. Place about one gallon of tepid water in an oversize bucket or similar container. Detergent may be added, but the additional cleaning effect is negligible, and residue from some detergents may cause corrosion.

2. Remove the gun barrel, if practical. Place one end in the bucket of water, and pump the water through the barrel using a workrod and oversize cleaning patch. If you can't remove the barrel, you may pour water through the barrel, allowing it to run out the nipple, and scrub with a patch and brush. Wrap old rags around the gun at the lock to pre-

Photo by Rick Hacker

NRA Staff Photo

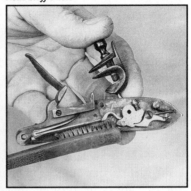

Muzzleloaders must be cleaned and oiled thoroughly after each use, or the excessive black powder fouling will attract moisture and cause corrosion.

vent the wood from being soaked. An alternative method is to use a cleaning kit that attaches a hose to the nipple hole; the other end of the hose is inserted in water, which is pumped through the barrel in a closed system.

The flintlock requires a little more effort. If the gun is particularly dirty, plug the flash hole with a round toothpick and fill the barrel about halfway with water or solvent. Let it soak for a few minutes, drain, and add a small amount of water. Use a patch to scrub the bore and then flush with water until clean. This may have to be repeated a couple of times to get the barrel completely clean.

3. Remove the lock and scrub fouling away with a toothbrush soaked in water or black powder solvent. Revolvers must be dismantled and cleaned.

4. Clean any fouling from the outside of the gun.

5. Wipe the bore and all parts of the gun dry, and set them aside to dry completely.

6. Oil the entire gun. Avoid using penetrating oil. Store in a dry place with fairly constant temperature.

Most field maintenance is cleaning related. A good black powder solvent and plenty of patches are essential to keep the muzzleloader working efficiently. Gun oil can be used to coat the barrel overnight or between hunting situations.

It's a good idea to remove and thoroughly clean the lock prior to going on a hunting trip. As dirt builds up in the lock, lock function slows. Use a good quality gun grease on bearing surfaces. The lock can be removed and cleaned in the field, though it is usually not necessary.

Tuning the Muzzleloader

You can better the performance and reliability of most muzzleloaders by tuning their mechanisms and making small modifications. For example, a flintlock can be tuned for faster ignition. A rifle's hammer or drum may be modified for more dependable ignition. Triggers of nearly all muzzleloaders may be adjusted for optimum weight of pull and minimum travel.

Before making such modifications, learn exactly what you need to do. Talk to a gunsmith or get professional instructions and diagrams for the procedure. If you don't, you may create a safety hazard or damage the firearm. Manufacturers usually recommend and give instructions for tuning. Problems resulting from major modifications to a gun are usually not covered under the manufacturer's warranty.

Photo by Mike Strandlund

Keep your muzzleloader in tune to prevent misfires and ensure peak performance.

CHAPTER 5

LOAD WORK-UP FOR RIFLES AND HANDGUNS

T he responsibilities inherent to hunting demand you develop the shooting skills and loads that make the surest, quickest kills. To be successful, muzzleloader hunters must make maximum use of their resources; to be responsible, they must know and abide by their limitations.

Photo by Rex Thomas

Get the most from your muzzleloader by developing, testing, and practicing with a variety of load combinations under controlled conditions.

The only way to develop shooting skill and get the most from a muzzleloader is through developing, testing, and practicing with different load combinations. With the great variance in load components, you need to do a lot of shooting to find the best combination. Along the way, you'll learn more about your gun, powder, and projectile, and improve your muzzleloader shooting ability.

What exactly constitutes a good hunting load and good muzzleloader marksmanship? A good load is first of all the most

95

accurate combination of components that provides sufficient energy and good bullet performance at hunting ranges. You may get best accuracy with a certain patched ball load in a .50-caliber rifle, but if you're hunting elk, its energy is dubious. You're better off switching to a slightly less accurate bullet with more energy and getting closer to the game. If you're hunting whitetails, for which either projectile would have sufficient energy, go with the better accuracy of the patched ball. Given various loads with equal accuracy, you should look at energy, trajectory, projectile expansion, speed of loading, and other considerations that constitute an effective hunting load.

Ballistics and Bullet Performance

The quickness and efficiency with which a projectile kills an animal depends on several factors. They include shot placement, the bullet's weight and velocity, and bullet performance.

Bullet placement is the most important factor. Any standard load will take a big game animal if it strikes the brain, forward part of the spinal column, or heart. Shots that solidly hit the lungs, liver, or a major blood vessel will most likely result in a quick kill. Shots in muscles or organs of moderate blood supply are marginal.

Whether these marginal shots will be quickly fatal depends largely on the load's energy and the bullet's dynamics on striking the animal. A bullet's energy is calculated by squaring the velocity (multiplying the velocity times itself) and multiplying that figure by the bullet's weight. If you double a bullet's weight, and keep velocity the same, you will double the energy. Double a bullet's velocity while keeping its weight the same, and energy increases fourfold. It is easy to see that velocity is twice as important as bullet weight in this formula, which is why smaller, high-velocity centerfire bullets are generally more lethal than muzzleloader projectiles.

There are other considerations besides the energy formula, however. The muzzleloader projectile, much heavier than a centerfire bullet, has more momentum for more penetration. If it strikes with enough force to deform itself, the bullet makes a larger wound channel inside the animal. Ideally for the hunter, the bullet will travel a long path though vital organs, expanding and imparting energy along the way, using up all its energy just as it leaves the animal. This assures that the most possible energy has been transferred to the target, there is a good wound channel,

Wildlife Management Institute Photos

The optimum hunting load depends on the size of the game, the closeness of your target, and other factors.

and there are two holes from which the game can leave a blood trail.

Experiments have shown that the impact of a projectile must be severe enough to cause significant projectile deformity in order to produce consistently quick kills. If the projectile does not hit hard enough to flatten, the bullet continues to travel through the tissue of the animal and may exit the opposite side without causing a mortal wound. This may be true in spite of good shot placement.

The minimum velocity at the point of impact that will achieve

97

adequate deformation of a round ball is around 1,250 feet per second. At less than 1,150 fps, the ball will not deform and will simply punch a small hole through the target animal. These statistics are for 100 percent pure lead balls; any alloy will greatly increase the amount of velocity needed for deformation.

To achieve 1,250 fps at the point of impact, the bullet must have muzzle velocity that is considerably higher. For instance, a .45-caliber ball must have a muzzle velocity of about 2,100 fps to retain enough velocity at 75 yards to deform. This requires the maximum recommended load.

The velocity necessary for deformation differs among bullet-shaped projectiles. Semi-hollowpoint bullets expand most reliably at normal hunting velocities.

Accuracy and Marksmanship

Accuracy is a function of marksmanship, firearm, and load. These should be developed to the point where 100 percent of your shots, under the conditions of hunting, are in an area equal to the vital zone of the animal you plan to hunt. For example, if you want to shoot offhand at a broadside deer 50 yards away, you should be able to keep all your shots in a circle about 10 inches in diameter at that range and position. If you want to shoot under the same conditions but at deer angling away, you'll have to keep all your shots in a vertical rectangle about 4 inches by 10 inches. If you can't keep bullet placement this precise, you must become a better marksman, develop a better load, or restrict your range.

As a general rule of muzzleloader accuracy, you should be able to shoot a two-inch group consistently from a benchrest and sandbags at 50 yards. While this does not simulate hunting conditions or requirements, it is a goal that is a good standard indicating accurate load and shooting ability. The benchrest is also the logical place to test components as you experiment to find the best load.

Some hunters can get acceptable hunting accuracy and performance from selecting a standard load for their rifle, sighting-in, and practicing. But true load workup is a science. It requires uniform shooting components, careful procedures, good notes, and precise marksmanship to result in a valid test. To make sure you are testing only the component and not your shooting ability or other factors, keep everything as constant as possible.

Photo by Mike Strandlund

Several variables affect the accuracy of a blackpowder load. Developing your shooting knowledge and experience will help you tighten your groups.

Benchrest Testing

Start with arranging gear: your rifle, various projectiles (both conicals and round balls), Pyrodex RS and FFg and FFFg black powder (check with manufacturer's recommendations), various patches and lubes, ball starter, ramrod, powder measure, spare nipples, and other tools and accessories. You'll also need a rock-solid bench and something to support your rifle (a mechanical rifle rest or heavy blocks and sandbags), targets, notepads and pencils, a slip-on pad or other recoil-dampening device, spotting scope or binoculars, and complete cleaning supplies. If you can, get a chronograph; it can be useful to compare velocities of different loads.

The type of target you use can make a difference in accuracy. Those with a fine cross and concentric circles are made for scopes, not open sights. Some muzzleloader shooters get best results with a heavy cross made of black tape on a buff background, such as the back of standard targets. Others prefer a black circle

NRA Staff Photo

Before heading to the shooting range, take inventory of all your necessary shooting and safety gear.

or square, about two or three inches across, which can be easier to align with a front sight.

If it's your first time shooting the rifle, start at about 10 yards to get the gun on target. A perfect zero is not necessary at this point; you'll be striving for small groups, not bullseyes. Then, since most hunters have an effective range of 50-100 yards, move your target to that range as the standard point for testing loads. Differences in accuracy among loads will be magnified and more apparent at this longer range.

Proper benchrest shooting technique is important for consistency. Best consistency is usually with an adjustable rifle-shooting pedestal with built-in pads front and rear. This device helps you hold the gun rock-steady for the truest test of gun and load rather than your shooting skills. If you have no pedestal, a good benchrest/sandbag arrangement can give about the same results. You'll need a solid support for the fore-end, such as a concrete block, and a half-dozen five- to 10-pound sandbags. The bags should be filled full enough that they stay firm, but not so firm that you cannot make grooves in the bags to support the rifle stock. Some shooters use bags of lead shot.

To set up and shoot from sandbags, put the block out in front, stack on a couple bags, and place a couple more bags on the bench where the buttstock will rest. Arrange the sandbags so the stock's fore-end (not the barrel itself) rests on the bags. The fore-end support should be in the same place you would hold it while hunting, and you should otherwise hold the rifle as you would in a hunting situation. Seat the rifle into the grooves of the sandbags as you align the sights on the bullseye. The set-up is correct when the sights are level and naturally aligned with the bullseye, and when they appear to move vertically to the

NRA Staff Photo

A legitimate comparison of various loads depends on precise bench-rest shooting procedure.

bullseye as you move the rifle forward and backward. If the rifle cants off-target as you move it back and forth, it means there is an uneven pressure, and a twisting backward recoil may vary bullet impact points. Finally, make sure your arrangement does not cause ramrod guides to catch on sandbags or cause stock abrasions.

As you shoot from this set-up, the bags should hold the sights on zero with no conscious effort on your part to put them on target. The sights should return to about zero after each shot. After a few shots, the sandbags may shift from recoil and need some adjustment. While the sandbags are holding the gun in alignment with the target, have a firm grip on the rifle to absorb recoil and simulate pressures you put on the stock in making a hunting shot. Unlike heavy benchrest guns, hunting muzzleloaders can lose accuracy with variance in pressure.

To test your gun and load accurately, you must do everything possible to minimize shooter error and other variables. Use a good target and set triggers if you have them. Ear and eye protection is a must, and recoil pads will improve your shooting ability. If it's windy, wait for calm. Even a slight breeze can affect the accuracy of the smaller muzzleloader bullets—especially patched balls. If you don't have confidence in your benchrest technique, practice until you do.

Before you shoot your first round, wipe all oil from the barrel, as this will change the point of impact of the first bullet and possibly the next. Put on eye and ear protection, clear the bench of debris (especially gunpowder), and take all other safety precautions. Refer to your gun owner's manual for other information before proceeding.

Load Development

The manual is also the best place to start your load development. Most manuals list minimum charges with various powders, projectiles, and calibers. Recommended maximum loads vary greatly, as much as 50 grains in the same caliber. This is because barrel and breech materials, construction, and thicknesses vary. While you need not start with the minimum listed load (these are usually too light to be used responsibly for hunting) you should adhere to the manufacturer's specs on maximum loads. Two general rules for load development are to start at about half the maximum load, or to load powder weight in grains (volume measure) equal to caliber (i.e. 50 grains for .50 caliber) with rifles of .45-.54 caliber. Some states have minimum powder loads that may be used for certain types of game.

The best powder charge depends on many variables. Some rifles shoot accurately over a wide range of powder charges, while others are more finicky. Some of the givens are these: Most rifles achieve best accuracy with around 70-90 percent of maximum load (for example, if the manufacturer states the maximum load for your gun is 120 grains, you'll probably get the best results with 100 grains or so). If you drop much below that, velocity drops off, trajectory increases, and other forces such as wind drift play a bigger role in affecting each shot. As you approach or exceed the maximum load, the powder may not burn completely before the bullet leaves the bore. This not only fills the barrel with residue, but affects accuracy; the high energies may damage load components, and the powder may burn to varying degrees with each shot. Also, as powder charges increase to a certain point, velocity often plateaus while recoil and breech pressure (along with powder expense) become unnecessarily high. Some shooters think of black powder as crude and tame compared to smokeless powder, but violent barrel explosions have been known to occur when breech pressures have been pushed too far.

When considering certain powder charges, make sure they are meant for the type of projectile you are considering. A standard patched ball can safely accept higher powder charges than large conical bullets in most cases because breech pressures are somewhat less with patched balls than with the heavier bullets.

Before starting your load workup, make a checklist of the

NRA Staff Photo

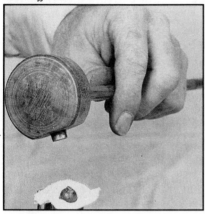

When testing loads, each charge must be inserted with care to maintain consistency. When loading molded balls, be sure to keep the sprue end up to ensure optimum accuracy.

components you want to test and the sequence of testing them. Develop a system of changing one component at a time while keeping all other variables constant, then moving on to test another component. Here is an example of a checklist for load workup:

Gun:	.50-caliber Thompson/Center Renegade
Sequence #1:	180-grain round ball, .015" patch, Crisco lube, Goex FFg black powder, 50,55,60, 65,70,80,85,90 grains; Pyrodex RS, same volumes.
Sequence #2:	250-grain REAL bullet, Crisco lube, Goex FFg black powder, 50,55,60,65,70,75,80 grains; Pyrodex RS, same volumes.

You may also want to develop a checklist of set-up, loading, and shooting steps to make sure nothing is forgotten or inadvertently changed.

After selecting your initial powder/bullet combination, load it carefully and put a mark on your ramrod at the muzzle. This ensures that you know when all similar loads are seated properly. Because you'll be changing loads, it's best to make this mark with pencil or tape, and make a permanent mark after you've selected your hunting load. Avoid making more than one mark on a ramrod at a time, to avoid hazardous confusion.

Shoot a three-shot group with your initial load, taking plenty of time between shots. When testing load combinations, it is important to space your shots out, shooting deliberately, to allow your barrel to cool. In a hunting situation, all your first shots

103

(normally your only shots) at game will be from a cold barrel. Because a barrel will change its points of impact as it heats up, you should approximate the hunting situation by letting the barrel cool as much as possible between shots. Wiping the barrel down with a wet rag will speed the process.

Your first shots at game will also be from a clean barrel, so use the cool-down time to wipe out the bore. This may be tedious, but it's necessary for consistency and to simulate hunting conditions; build-up of residue will affect your rifle's accuracy. A brass brush or brush/cloth works fine, or you can use a solvent-soaked patch. If you are doing extensive shooting, also clean the bolster/flash hole and scrape residue from the tip of the breech plug, where there may be build-up that you can't remove with a brush or patch.

If you're testing many loads, it's best to shoot a good three-shot group of each load combination and then go back to confirm your favorite loads. A "good" group is one that you're sure hasn't been affected by shooter error, a wind gust, or other factors not related to the load chain.

Keep Notes

Write down notes on each load combination before progressing to the next.

Records should include the following:

- **Specific gun and caliber**
- **Powder type, make, granulation, and volume**
- **Type and size of patch and/or lubricant**
- **Distance from target**
- **Group size (measuring the widest-spread holes, from the near side of one to the far side of the other)**
- **Location of group relative to the bullseye**
- **Range conditions (wind, precipitation)**
- **Loading and shooting procedure**
- **Date**
- **Velocity (if you have a chronograph)**
- **Penetration, expansion data, if tested.**

This information can be written on the targets themselves, which also preserves a graphic reference of your groups, but keeping the data in a notebook makes later review more convenient.

After shooting a good group with your initial load, test another by changing one component at a time. If you start with a .50-caliber rifle at 50 grains of FFg, move up to 55 grains of the

Photo by Peter Schoonmaker

Many shooters like to jot down load data right on the target, which keeps written notes and a graphic record together.

same powder, keeping the projectile, patch, lube, tamping pressure, and everything else the same.

Increase the powder charge by five-grain increments, shooting a three-shot group at each level, until you approach the maximum load. If, reviewing your notes, you notice an unusually wide group, you may want to try it again to see if shooter error or another factor was involved. Then start over, using a different powder, bullet, or patch, going through all the levels of powder charge.

Refining Loads

For round balls, the tightness of the patch is often the biggest factor affecting accuracy of a load. Try patches of different thicknesses and materials, retrieving and examining patches that have been shot downrange. Check for holes and tears, which could hurt accuracy and suggest more careful loading or a stronger patch material. If the patch appears burned or charred, it is probably too thin and is allowing too much gas to blow through. Since you'll be shooting in the field, make sure to discard any patch material that smolders or catches fire.

In testing conical bullets, try a wide variety of designs, sizes, and lubrications. Normally, the tightest-fitting conical is the most accurate, but not always. Even if your gun is designed for a certain type of bullet, you may get better accuracy with another. For example, long, slow-twist barrels are designed for good round ball accuracy over a wide range of velocities, but they may also shoot shorter bullets well.

During your component testing, also test your gun's reliability of ignition. Stick with one brand of cap unless you have a misfire attributable to the cap; then try another. With a flintlock, try to find the most reliable way of fitting and knapping the flint and priming the pan.

Once you've got your most accurate load combinations narrowed down, try slight variations on each, seeing if you can further refine the accuracy of a certain load by tamping it differently or making some other minor change. Then compare the other performance considerations of your most accurate loads. Is trajectory the main concern? Then try your loads at various ranges to find the flattest-shooting powder/bullet combination. Need more downrange energy? Then the larger conical bullets are your best bet, though trajectory will probably suffer, and you'll have to further restrict your range. Want the closest thing to pioneer hunting traditions? Then you'll want the patched ball.

Since higher velocity gives a bullet more game-taking energy and flatter trajectory, you may want to hunt with the highest-velocity load that is still safe and accurate. It is not advisable to guess which is the fastest load by the amount of powder used, because velocity plateaus and even falls as powder charges become too great. It can be very helpful to measure the velocity of your bullets with a chronograph as you develop loads. Chronographs are available at some sports shops and gun clubs, and have become more affordable in recent years.

It's also a good idea to examine the penetration and expansion of various bullets at various ranges. Round balls, hollowpoint conicals, and heavy solid bullets have varying terminal ballistics. You can test these by shooting into wet phone books, soft wood, or other such material.

Zeroing the Rifle

After selecting a hunting load, it's time to zero the rifle. Determine your effective hunting range and zero your rifle there. Most experts recommend sighting-in an open-sighted muzzleloader at your maximum accurate shooting distance and then testing the point of impact at closer ranges. Your shots will probably be a bit high at mid range and a bit low very close, but

Photo by Mike Strandlund

Many guns and loads can be sighted-in at very short range and still be on zero at more distant hunting ranges. Most will hit the bullseye at about 12 yards, rise an inch or two at 40-50, and fall back to hit the bullseye again at about 75 yards. Be sure to test rather than guess the trajectory of your loads.

they should be well within the vital region of a deer-sized animal. Small game hunters must zero their firearms more precisely and be aware of yardage adjustments that may be necessary.

For quicker initial zeroing of a muzzleloader, begin shooting at close range—about 12 yards from the target. Adjust to hitting the bullseye at that yardage, then test your shooting at your maximum accurate range. Chances are your range will be around 75 yards with a good rest, and your gun zeroed at 12 yards will shoot right-on at that range after shooting just a little high at 50 yards. The flatter-shooting loads will be just a bit low at 90-100 yards, but heavier, slower bullets will require a higher hold on a big game target. With a sight-in system like this, most muzzleloader hunters should not have to worry about trajectory when shooting within their effective range. Because each type of load will vary, test your shooting at all yardages so you know for sure where the point of impact is at each distance.

Zeroing a modern muzzleloader with screw-adjustable sights is a simple matter of moving the rear sight in the direction you want to move your shots (move the sight up if you want to shoot higher, left if you want to move your shots left). The same principle applies to fixed-dovetail sights, but more care is needed; these front or rear sights must be tapped for horizontal movement. Vertical adjustment usually requires filing either sight,

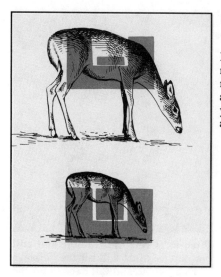

If you have developed your marksmanship skills, long range (100–125 yards) shots are possible. Depending on your load, you may have to adjust your sight picture.

but some shooters prefer to change elevation by changing their sight picture to ensure they don't file their sights beyond adjustment for some future change.

The best sight picture for open buckhorn-style sights is the center hold, centering the tip of the front sight at the bottom of the exact spot you want to hit. Some shooters who use bullets with a substantial trajectory or who can shoot accurately at longer ranges compensate for trajectory by changing the sight picture. For example, at 50 yards the front sight may be just visible in the deepest point of the notch, while at 100 yards it may be even with the shelf of the rear sight (see illustration). To be successful with this method, you must be a good judge of distance and have a solid mental picture of what your sights should look like at different ranges.

Once a satisfactory hunting load is established, a hunter needs to shoot that particular combination at several distances. This discloses where the shot will hit in relationship to the line of sight at different ranges. Once in the hunting area, distances to different landmarks can be paced off or measured with an optical rangefinder to give the hunter a comparison marker for estimating game distances. Shot placement can then be adjusted for trajectory. For instance, a common trajectory for a muzzleloading rifle loaded with a round ball will place a shot directly on the line of sight at 12½ yards and at 75 yards, place it a couple inches higher at 25 to 50 yards, and let it drop a few inches at 100 yards.

Another important step in testing your load is to shoot it at a steep angle. Bullets shot at severe uphill or downhill angles impact higher than they would when shot at the same distance on the level. Most affected by angles are slow, heavy bullets shot at longer ranges. This means that a muzzleloader hunter shooting on a slope or from a tree stand could miss the mark by several inches if he does not take this factor into account and know how to compensate.

Handgun Load Workup

The same principles used in working up a load for a rifle apply to pistols. They involve testing variables by changing one thing at a time, keeping everything else the same, including your rock-solid hold.

When benchrest shooting a handgun, be sure again not to rest the barrel—just the butt and the triggerguard/frame should touch the sandbags. Shoot at a reasonable pistol-shooting distance—about 30 yards is maximum, and much closer is more realistic—because of the small targets you'll be hunting and the relatively inaccurate gun you're using.

With a revolver, load workup is simpler because there are fewer variables. The charge is limited to the amount of powder that will fit in the chamber, and projectiles are limited to round balls or perhaps very short conicals. Revolvers generally shoot

Photo by Rex Thomas

The principles for load development and practice are the same for a pistol as for a rifle. Since hunting pistols are suitable only for small and medium-size game, variances in bullet energy have little significance but accuracy is crucial.

better groups with lighter loads, because the balls may strip through the rifling with heavier loads. However, handgun accuracy depends more on practice than load development.

Marksmanship Development

To get the most out of your accurate load and straight-shooting firearm, you must practice shooting. This means working on the fundamentals of marksmanship, detailed in Chapter 4, until you're satisfied with the level of ability you have atttained. Then continue to practice regularly to maintain and fine-tune your shooting skill.

Quality practice is important. Just shooting a lot is not good enough—for your shooting skill to improve, you must master marksmanship fundamentals and concentrate on making each shot your best. Incorrect practice only reinforces your mistakes.

As you practice, shoot under the conditions you would have in hunting—wear hunting clothes, use practical hunting positions, and practice in a safe, woodsy setting. As you practice, visualize actual hunting situations. It will motivate you to shoot better and prepare you mentally for a game-shooting situation. Use lifesize game targets or outlines of vital areas to determine your effective accurate range.

When you are unable to shoot live ammunition, you can practice by dry-firing in your home. *First, be especially sure the gun is unloaded.* Set up targets such as animal pictures that you can "shoot" at with your unloaded gun. To protect the lock parts, place a buffer between your gun's hammer and nipple or frizzen. A rubber or leather pad works well. Flintlock shooters can also use a piece of wood in the shape of a flint for dry-firing.

Photo by Dave Messics

Practicing from various distances and positions will prepare you best for shooting situations in the field.

CHAPTER 6

LOAD WORK-UP FOR SHOTGUNS

While a muzzleloading rifle or pistol is quite a different creature from its centerfire counterpart, the blackpowder shotgun nearly equals the modern scattergun in field performance. The main drawback is the muzzleloader's slowness to reload, which is usually not a material factor when using a double-barrel. A smoothbore muzzleloader can be loaded to copy the load performance of almost any shotshell, and can be very effective at taking small game and birds, waterfowl, medium-size game like turkeys and coyotes, and even deer.

As in all shooting, the blackpowder shotgunner must gain full knowledge of his gun's operation and skill in its use. Load development, testing, and practice are even more important with a muzzleloading shotgun, because more variables are involved.

Photo by Mike Strandlund

A careful shooter can work up blackpowder shotgun loads that are on par with modern loads in energy, patterning, and overall game-taking capability.

The hunter must find the right size and amount of pellets and the optimum amount of powder. He must know the best procedure for loading. He must know where the shotgun shoots and how it patterns. He must practice until he becomes adept at handling and shooting it in the field.

Shotgun Load Requirements

Components of a blackpowder shotgun load include a cap or flint ignition system, the powder charge, wads and cards, and pellets. The right combination of components must be used to ensure the most desirable load for the game being hunted. The principles of modern shotgun loads also apply to blackpowder shotgunning; the powder charge, pellet size and weight, and pattern must match the game and distances you shoot.

The game-taking ability of a shotgun load depends on two factors: pellet energy in relation to the size of the game, and the number of pellets that find their mark. Ideally, three to six pellets, heavy enough and moving fast enough to penetrate internal organs and break wing bones, will strike the vital zone of the target. More than this, and meat damage will be too high; less, and the game may escape.

As the pellet charge leaves the shotgun muzzle, pellets spread out and slow down. For very close-range shooting, lighter loads and a wider pellet spread, or pattern, is desirable to minimize meat destruction and maximize chances of hitting the target. At longer ranges, the hunter needs more pellets, heavier pellets, and a tighter-flying pattern to retain the effectiveness of the shot.

As a general rule for shooting at longer ranges, it is more important to achieve multiple hits than high per-pellet energy. A shotgun shot tends to lose effectiveness more from the pattern spreading too thin than from pellets losing energy. In other words, it is better to have tight patterns with more pellets of a smaller size than to use larger pellets and hope for a lucky hit from a blown pattern.

Larger game like geese requires larger-size shot driven at high velocity to ensure there is enough energy in multiple hits to incapacitate the animal. Smaller game like doves require denser patterns to be sure that pellets reach the small vital areas, with lesser requirements of velocity, which means pellet size and powder charge are smaller. Tighter chokes are needed for longer-range shooting or especially tough game like turkeys or coyotes, while the open chokes are best for close shooting at flushed birds and rabbits.

Photo by Stan Warren

Photo by Rick Hacker

The size of the game and the shooting situation determine the appropriate shotgun load. Small, fast-flushing upland birds require wide patterns with a dense swarm of small pellets; tough turkeys need tighter patterns of larger shot.

The powder and pellet charge, pellet size, and pattern type can be manipulated for the best load for a certain game under certain circumstances. Refer to the load-workup table and recommended load table for starting points. Then experiment on patterning paper and in the field to determine your best load.

There is a time-honored formula called volume for volume used to determine the correct charge for blackpowder shotgunning. With this method, you use the same volumes of powder and shot—typically with a powder measure set on 70-100 grains. In using this method, be aware that it is *volume* for *volume*, or bulk for bulk. Do not use equal weights. If this formula does

113

not produce satisfactory patterns, using a slightly higher ratio of pellets to powder may make an improvement.

Pellets

Pellets used by the blackpowder shotgunner are the same used in modern shotguns. Usually sold in 25-pound bags, the more commonly used pellets range in size from buckshot suitable for deer to number 9 shot, used for clay targets and the smallest game birds.

Shot is manufactured to different degrees of hardness. Pure lead shot is the softest and the most easily deformed in the barrel by pressure from the ramrod, the push of the powder ignition, or the sides of the barrel. Chilled shot (lead shot alloyed with antimony) and copper-coated lead shot provide greater shape stability than regular lead shot. Some regions require the use of steel shot or non-toxic shot for waterfowling. If steel shot must be used in a particular hunting area, a non-toxic shot cup large enough to hold the entire shot charge is required to protect your barrel from permanent scoring damage. Always follow the manufacturer's recommendations.

Shotgun Powder

The black powder used in shotguns is generally coarser than that used in rifles. While the rifleman may use FFFg in small- and medium-bore guns, the shotgunner should use only FFg, Fg, or Pyrodex RS. The reason is that shotgun barrels and breeches are thinner than those of rifles. It is safer to use a coarser granulation that produces less breech pressure. A slower ignition and gentler "push" is also less likely to deform pellets, which hurts a shotgun pattern's effectiveness.

Wads and Cards

The type of wads and cards you use in a shotgun load will affect the pattern of the load. There are several types of each available. Wads are made in varying thicknesses—usually the heavier the load, the thicker the wad. Wads are usually made from a cushiony material such as insulation board, and cards are typically cardboard.

Wads are available from muzzleloading arms suppliers or can be made at home by the budget-conscious shooter.

In general, use three times as much wadding between the powder and shot as you use over the shot. The reason for this is to keep the powder charge from burning through the wad

114

Photo by Dwain Bland

Photo by Mike Strandlund

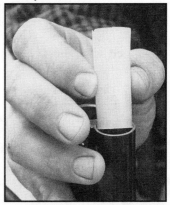

Hornet's nest (left) is a traditional shotgun wadding material. Shooters tend to get more consistency with modern components such as plastic shot cups (right) which are more uniform and allow for tighter patterning. Make sure the cup fits well and that there is no build-up of plastic fouling in the bore.

during ignition. If the over-powder wad is burned through, hot gases will push through the shot, spreading the pattern unevenly and wasting energy. Many shooters like to use a thick felt wad or fiber cushion wad to soften the impact of the powder ignition on the shot charge. This makes for less shot deformity and consequently a better pattern. A cushion wad is fairly light and porous, though, and it is likely to burn through unless a stout cardboard wad is seated between it and the powder charge. The thinnest over-shot card capable of holding the load together reliably will probably result in the best pattern.

The simplest cards can be cut by hand out of ³⁄₃₂-inch cardboard. Precut cardboard wads are also available from most blackpowder accessories outlets. Either way, use two wads or a double thickness wad over the powder charge and a single thickness over the shot load.

In some cases, muzzleloading shotgunners get good results using some modern shotshell components. Plastic shot cups, perhaps with a cushioned wad, are often the best way to achieve a very tight pattern. Whether you can get good results with a shot cup depends on your gun, because bore diameters of various shotguns differ slightly within each gauge. The cup may fit snugly in the bore of one 12-gauge, and too loosely in another. A loose load can be a safety hazard and let gas leak around the pellet charge, causing a loss of velocity. Another problem is that plastic fouling can accumulate quickly in the bore when using any kind of plastic components in blackpowder shooting, requiring the shooter to clean after each shot.

Plastic shot cups should be loaded over a snugly fitting cushioned wad, empty, with the shot added next, followed by an over-shot wad or card.

Load Experimentation

The number of variables that go into finding the right load for a particular hunting situation are numerous and can get confusing if they're considered all at once. However, the seemingly endless possibilities begin to look manageable when they are considered in small groups or categories.

The blackpowder shotgun shooter must work up loads carefully for the sake of safety and consistency. There are several basic steps of loading a blackpowder shotgun for hunting.

First, determine the performance you need from your load. Most important, it must be safe to shoot; check with recommendations from the gun's manufacturer. If they are not available, play it safe and do not use loads any stronger than those listed here.

Keeping your load within safe parameters, you must match the load to the game and the shooting conditions. For each game species, there are standard pellet sizes, powder charges, and pattern characteristics established. But the same species can be hunted under greatly varying conditions, and the load should be the right one for those conditions. For example, ducks can be hunted over decoys at close range; by jump-shooting at medium range, and by pass-shooting a maximum range. The best loads and patterning performance are different in each situation. Check the accompanying table for starters.

While a shooter can only calculate the optimum pellet and powder charge, he can actually test his patterns. Before you begin your shotgun load development, make some paper cutouts approximating the vital area of the game you'll hunt. Later, you can shoot loads at a piece of paper, hold the template over the pellet pattern, and determine the range where the pattern is effective for the game you are hunting.

Assemble a variety of shotgun components—two or three sizes of pellets and wads—for each type of game you hunt. You may want to try FFg and Fg black powder and Pyrodex RS; the difference in their pressures can have an impact on the consistency of patterns. Remember throughout your test-shooting that varying any of these components will produce different results. Differences in packing the load will also change the way it shoots. Keep careful notes as you develop loads so you know the exact set of variables that gives best results.

Your early testing will be on stationary patterning paper only. You need a safe backstop, a clear shooting lane of about 45 yards (the maximum recommended shooting range), a mount for your patterning sheet, and a bench rest or other steady rest.

To test patterns, you need paper at least 30 inches square—40 is better. Butcher paper or brown wrapping paper is good patterning paper. Newsprint can work, but pellet holes are harder to see. Some shooters use plywood, whitewashing it with a paint roller after each shot. You may also use NRA Life-Size Game Targets.

Set up the patterning sheet vertically and mark an aiming

Photo by Rick Hacker

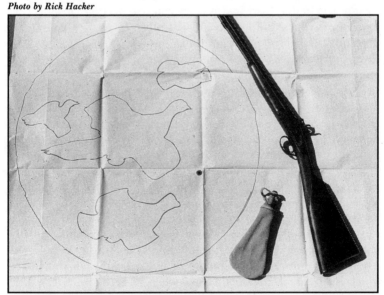

The most reliable test of a shotgun pattern is to count pellet hits within outlines of the game you plan to shoot. Be sure to consider only the vital zones of the animal outlines.

point. While patterning, you will also be testing how well the shotgun centers the pattern on the point of aim. Step off the yardage you want to test, normally between 15 and 45 yards.

Choose a load from the shotgun maker's recommendations, or from another reliable source, being sure to use pellets that are large enough for the game you'll hunt. Use eye and ear protection. Load carefully, hold steadily on the aiming point, and fire.

Take down the patterning sheet and examine it. Find the center of the pattern, and mark it. How does that center of impact compare with the aiming point? It shouldn't be more than three or four inches off, or it could pose an accuracy problem. If you're using a double-barrel, don't make any adjustments for changing impact point until you've tested both barrels. If they shoot much differently, you may need the help of a gunsmith.

Check the density and consistency of the pattern. The pattern should not be too thin, or have "holes" or gaps where no pellets hit. Using the template of your game's vital area, check to see that there is no place in the pattern where the cutout will fit without sufficient pellet hits. The very minimum number of hits for an acceptable load is three. If you are getting close to this minimum, you should do a lot of testing to ensure your load does not fall below that minimum.

If your load can't make minimum standards, you have several options. You can shorten the range, use a heavier load (as long as it doesn't exceed maximum load) or you can try to tighten the pattern.

Tightness of the pattern is controlled by several factors, largely by the shotgun's muzzle configuration. Most muzzleloading shotguns and muskets have a straight muzzle called cylinder bore, in which the bore is the same diameter from breech to muzzle. To get a tighter pellet pattern, the shotgun muzzle may be narrowed, or choked. The common chokes, from most open to narrowest, include improved cylinder, modified, and full. At least one gunmaker offers screw-in choke tubes on a muzzleloading shotgun, which allows the shooter to vary his pellet pattern. Another technique to manipulate pellet pattern is the jug choke, which is a bulge in the bore a few inches from the muzzle, which also causes a tighter pattern. While conventional chokes may make it a bit difficult to load some wads, the jug choke prevents the problem.

Many double-barrel shotguns have each tube choked differently. This gives the shooter a more open pattern for a close shot, then a tighter follow-up pattern as the missed target or additional targets gain distance.

Along with choke, the pattern density will be determined by several other factors. Smaller shot normally spreads more; if you want a tighter pattern, moving up a size or two can help. Damage to pellets also causes them to spread more. This shot deformation results from the powder explosion, pellets compressing and striking each other, and from pellets striking and scraping the bore wall. Undamaged pellets make a tighter pattern. This can be accomplished by a coarser powder granulation, which burns slower and results in slower pellet acceleration. Good wads also minimize pellet deformation, and wadding techniques can change the pattern considerably. More wads behind the shot tend to tighten the pattern, while more in front of the shot tend to make it spread. Be careful in your use of wads, however. The extra mass and increased sealing of more wads or heavier wads will increase breech pressure. A plastic shot cup will not only minimize damage to pellets, but keep them together for an extra fraction of a second as they leave the bore, helping tighten the pattern.

Rating Patterns

Try different components and procedures in developing the pattern that is right for the hunting situation you anticipate. To compare loads, you may determine the percentage of pellets that are striking in an effective pattern. First, you must know the approximate number of pellets in a certain load (measure and count them). Then shoot a pattern at a measured distance, locate the center of impact, and draw a 30-inch circle around this center. You can use a template circle or make a compass by driving a tack through a strip of wood and drilling a hole 15 inches from the tack. To draw the circle, place the tack in the center of impact, insert a pencil point in the hole, and pivot the pencil around the tack. Count the number of pellets within the circle. To determine the percentage of pellets that are striking in that 30-inch circle, multiply the number of hits by 100, then divide by the total number of pellets in the load. For example, if there were 220 pellets in the load and you had 143 hits, the formula would be 143 x 100 = 14,300, divided by 220 = 65, or 65 percent.

Standard patterning for rating the patterns of certain guns is done at 40 yards with 30-inch circles. The practical hunter is more interested in actual anticipated shooting yardages, however, and he realizes that pattern percentages are for comparing patterns against each other. The ultimate test for the hunting shotgunner is with vital-zone templates. Minor changes in powder charges, wads, and loading procedures can change how the shotgun patterns. Experiment—within the realms of safety, of course.

In the case of a muzzleloading shotgun pattern that is "blown," or full of holes, the problem usually lies in powder or wad. Try using Fg black powder. Try a tighter wad, or a different card behind it to prevent the hot gasses from leaking through or past the wad. You may also try decreasing your powder charge or increasing your pellet charge.

Generally you can get a tighter pattern by using less powder and more shot, or by using a plastic cup or better cushion wad. Widen a pattern by inserting an extra card within the pellet charge, or by using a heavier powder charge.

Never assume that your adjustments to the load has accomplished what was intended. Always pattern-test a new load.

Pellet Velocity and Penetration

You can test pellet penetration at the same time you pattern your loads. A rough but accurate guide to effective penetration can be tested with old phone books or magazines. Shoot into a solidly supported book at 25 yards and measure penetration by counting the number of pages each particular load penetrates. Sufficient penetration for smaller game like grouse is about one-eighth inch, from the surface of the book to the imbedded pellet. Loads for larger game like ducks should penetrate a quarter-inch.

You can increase pellet penetration by using larger pellets, a smaller load of pellets, or stronger powder charge. Do not exceed maximum charges, however—it is unsafe and will not provide the desired results. Beyond a certain powder charge, velocity levels off and actually falls, because the entire powder charge cannot burn before the pellets leave the bore. In that case, the excess powder becomes useless mass that absorbs energy rather than creates it.

A chronograph can also reveal valuable information on shot load velocities.

Shotgun Practice

Once you've determined a good load for your shotgun and shot some paper, it's time to practice on moving targets. Trap and skeet fields are fine, but the best shotgun practice for a hunter is with clay birds flying in a setting that matches hunting surroundings. This is particularly true for hunters of upland birds. Practice shooting in a woods—either an established sporting clays course or a makeshift course in a safe area using portable clay target traps.

In general, percussion blackpowder shotguns have a lock and ignition time lapse close to that of modern shotguns, but a little change in shooting technique may be required. A snap-shooter, aiming at a point in space in front of the bird, or a swing-through shooter swinging up from behind and past the bird, may have to modify his timing. A sustained-lead shooter with good follow-through should not have to change his lead or timing.

Flintlocks usually have a significantly longer time lapse between trigger pull and pellet departure. Most shotgunners find they must significantly change their wingshooting technique with a flintlock.

NRA Staff Photo

After developing a load that patterns well for flying game birds, practice shooting on moving targets. Experienced centerfire shotgun shooters may find they have to adjust their lead or timing somewhat when shooting a muzzleloader.

Shotgun Loads for Muzzleloader Hunters		
Game	**Pellet charge**	**Powder charge**
Coyote, turkey	1-½ oz BB	90 grs. FFg
Goose, large duck	1-⅜ oz. steel BB	90 grs FFg
Medium-size duck	1-¼ oz steel #2	80 grs FFg
Pheasant, grouse	1-¼oz lead #6	80 grs FFg
Squirrel, rabbit	1-⅛ oz lead #6	70 grs FFg
Quail, woodcock, dove	1-⅛ oz lead #7 ½	70 grs FFg

The above chart gives recommended 12-gauge loads for various game under common hunting conditions. The shot size and powder charge should increase if shots are at maximum range. Loads will increase or decrease by about 20 percent if a 10-gauge or 20-gauge are used.

Buckshot and Slugs

Some muzzleloader hunters use buckshot for larger game up to deer size. The application of these loads is very limited, however. In most areas buckshot is not legal for deer. Heavy buckshot loads are not safe in many blackpowder shotguns. The range of such loads on deer-size game is very restricted—about 25 yards is tops.

Like all shotgun loads, buckshot should be pattern-tested before it is taken hunting. The best buckshot patterns usually come from open chokes and buffered loads—loads in which padding takes up the large gaps between pellets, minimizing their deformation. Cream of Wheat cereal is a commonly used buffer in blackpowder shotguns.

Buckshot patterns suitable for deer hunting are difficult to develop. You must have at least three vital-area hits per shot to qualify as a good load, using buckshot of at least .32 caliber (number 0). An average buckshot load will have between eight and 15 pellets. Check with manufacturer recommendations before loading buckshot, and check with local regulations before hunting with it.

The use of solid slugs in muzzleloading shotguns is not recommended. The shotgun's smooth bore and crude bead sight very seldom can lead to accuracy acceptable for hunting big game, and the thin-walled breech prohibits the use of high-energy loads.

Part III

How to Hunt with a Muzzleloader

Photo by Mike Strandlund

CHAPTER 7
BIG GAME HUNTING

I t may sound peculiar, but muzzleloader hunting has skyrocketed in popularity for two opposing reasons: It makes big game hunting harder—and easier.

After many seasons, some people become bored with hunting. But take a routine hunting trip, add a dash of black powder, and it becomes a new, exciting challenge. On the other hand, many states have opened special blackpowder seasons that, because they give you more time to hunt or a *better* time to hunt,

Photo by Rick Hacker

Hunting is more challenging with a muzzleloader than a modern rifle, which makes success more difficult—but sweeter. Special big game seasons often give blackpowder hunters a certain advantage over the regular-season throngs.

Photo by Joe Workosky

You'll have to put together all your big game hunting, shooting, and woodsmanship skills to be successful with a muzzleloader.

give you more chance each year to tag your buck or bull.

Whatever the attraction, you'll have to put together all your hunting, shooting, and woodsmanship skills to be successful with a muzzleloader. In blackpowder hunting for big game, most effective shots are made at less than 50 yards. This means you'll probably have to pass up most of the animals you see. Your hunting skills will be tested to the limit as you try to get very near the game to make your one shot count. It will probably be much more difficult than the hunting you're used to. But the quest is more exciting and success is more fulfilling. Give blackpowder hunting for big game an honest try, and you'll probably be hooked forever.

The Big Game Blackpowder Gun

The choice of muzzleloading rifles for big game is a much-debated question. Some hunters have definite views on which types of guns and loads are appropriate for certain kinds of game. Often these views are misguided.

Many factors contribute to whether a certain gun and load will be effective for a certain animal. Very important are range and bullet placement. If the game is close enough and the shot hits the heart, upper spine, or both lungs, bullet energy require-

Photo by Mike Strandlund

The big game hunter has many options in caliber, powder charge, and projectile to choose from. Making the right choice may be critical to your success.

ments are not as great as when the shot strikes a less-vital area such as the liver or a major blood vessel. If the shot misses both primary and secondary vital areas, no gun will be enough for a quick kill.

Generally, minimum requirements for hunting big game with a muzzleloader are .50 caliber for deer and .54 caliber for anything bigger. Depending on circumstances, a light load may do; or, you may need a very heavy powder charge, a conical bullet, or some other ingredient to meet minimum requirements.

Keep in mind that the potency of these blackpowder loads are usually far less than accepted modern centerfire loads for big game. Don't be fooled by a cavernous bore; velocity is the most important factor in a bullet's energy, and muzzleloaders produce comparatively low velocity.

As an example, many hunters have the impression that a .50-caliber muzzleloader is an adequate elk rifle. It may be with a precise shot at very close range. But at 50 yards, even the fastest .50-caliber conicals have well under *half* the energy of a .30-06 bullet, which is considered by many experts to be a minimum modern load for elk. Obviously, marginal placement of that conical can only lead to disaster. A famous phrase bears repeating: Use enough gun.

Guns and loads are discussed further under each species heading later in this chapter.

Preparing for a Blackpowder Hunt

Planning a big game hunt with a muzzleloader involves a lot of

Photo by Mike Strandlund   *Photo by Gerald Almy*

Scouting and planning play a big part in the outcome of a muzzleloader hunt. Find where the big bucks are and get the lay of the land well before it's time to hunt.

the same preparation that goes into any big game hunt. There are considerations involving guns, gear, and special tactics. The more you know about a particular kind of big game, the better your chances will be for success with a muzzleloader.

Seasons

Many states have separate muzzleloader seasons for big game animals. Sometimes these fall before the modern-gun seasons and sometimes after. The table in this book's appendix was prepared from information given by game departments. Double check all seasons and dates with the most current regulations of your state or province before you plan your hunt. Planning should begin as early as possible; if you're hunting out of state, a year and a half in advance is not too soon. It may take longer than that to draw a permit.

Studying the Game Animals

After you've decided what and when to hunt, the next step is to learn as much as you can about the animal's general behavior and its preferred habitat. All big game animals have certain

Photo by Gerald Almy   *Photo by Richard P. Smith*

One of his most valuable skills is a hunter's ability to spot hard-to-see game. Train your eye, and use high-quality binoculars.

behavior patterns that the hunter can use in planning hunting strategy. Each type of big game animal has certain preferred habitat, as well as habits for bedding, feeding, and traveling. Most change their habitat and food preferences with the seasons. For example, whitetails may be found each evening on crop fields early in the season, but may stay in oak groves as acorns ripen later in the fall. Most big game in mountainous regions migrate. They summer high in the mountains just above or below timberline. When the weather changes—usually during the early part of the hunting season—they move into lower elevations to avoid deep snows. This movement directly relates to weather, not just time of year. In some years the animals may still be on

The best possible big game shot for the muzzleloader hunter is the point just below the mid-line of the animal's body and behind the shoulder. Try to avoid anything but a two-lung shot.

summer range in muzzleloader season while in other years a storm may have already pushed them much lower. If they are on the move, in strange terrain, animals may be warier. Conversely, the migration will often coincide with rutting seasons, when the behavior of bucks and bulls changes drastically and they become more vulnerable. During that time, you can apply special knowledge and tactics to outsmart an otherwise unapproachable animal.

Know Your Hunting Area

During blackpowder seasons, public lands are often less crowded than they will be during the modern gun season.

How much you know about your hunting area will greatly increase your chances with a muzzleloader, because you'll understand about landforms and points critical to the location and movements of game. Whether you plan to hunt near home or out of state, get topographic maps of the hunting area.

Well before hunting season starts, make some scouting trips into your planned hunting area. Look for sign made by the animals you seek, such as tracks, trails, droppings, scrapes, and wallows. Look for landforms and habitat that will attract game. Dense cover, rock slides, watering areas, passes, and access points will help you find points where animals pass as they move between resting, watering, and feeding spots. Consider other factors like hunter pressure and accessibility. Decide on several stand locations, and consider strategies you might use to still-hunt or drive certain pieces of cover.

Even if you hunt near home, you may be tempted to choose the most remote areas with the idea that game there will be less disturbed and more plentiful. This may not be true. The characteristics of the range, the size of the area, and accessibility problems may mean that you never see an animal at all. For your first time in a new area, a guided hunt may be the best choice.

Extended Hunting Trips

Most hunters do much of their hunting close to home, and take an occasional long-distance hunting trip. Out-of-state excursions require considerable planning, and their success is often proportional to the amount of preparation the hunter does.

Game departments are a good source of general information for nonresident hunters. Learn about possible hunting areas so you can pick the hunting site that offers the most of what you're looking for in the way of game, terrain, etc. Check all state

Photo by Jim Zumbo

Photo by Mike Strandlund

Photo by Jim Zumbo

Photo by Rex Thomas

Among the various approaches to muzzleloader big game hunting include RV/tent camping, day trips, horse-packing with an outfitter, and backpacking.

or provincial information carefully for application deadline dates and fees.

When an American hunts in Canada, or vice-versa, he needs to remember customs regulations. To save time at the border, have a list of all your equipment and any serial numbers. You may need proof on your return that you did not purchase these items in Canada, or else you will have to pay import duty. Generally, a blackpowder rifle and 50 rounds of ammunition can be taken duty-free into Canada. Handguns are not allowed.

Hiring an Outfitter

Blackpowder hunters tend to be independent, but time may not allow you to become as well acquainted with your game and hunting area as you need to be. A professional outfitter or guide can make the difference. Get a listing of outfitters and guides by contacting game departments, by checking ads in outdoor magazines, or by contacting NRA Hunter Services Division. After

making your list, contact each and ask about special arrange-
ments for blackpowder hunts. The outfitter should be professional and supply you with information on packaged hunts,
prices, and a detailed list of services he provides.

Be sure you understand how many hunters will be in the party
per guide, and ask for a list of references. Before you decide on
an outfitter, be sure there is a signed agreement and that all
costs, including deposit, are in writing. No guide can guarantee
a trophy or good weather, but careful planning and a signed
agreement will minimize misunderstandings and help ensure a
pleasant hunt.

Personal Preparation

Get into shape before the hunt, and give yourself a chance to
adjust to changes in altitude and terrain. You cannot afford to
be out of breath and shaking from fatigue when it's time to
shoot. Also remember to try out your clothes, gear, and other
equipment and accessories before taking them into the field. A
hard hunt far from the nearest trading post is no place to find

Photo by Mike Strandlund

**If you're a little out of shape or embarking
on a strenuous hunt, physical preparation
will make your trip much more enjoyable.**

boots are too tight, your poncho is too noisy, or your percussion
caps are the wrong size.

The way you dress can have a major impact on the comfort,
safety, and success of your hunt. Dress in layers so that you are
prepared for morning and evening cold and midday warmth.
Have raingear available if there's any chance of showers. Select
your hat according to its ability to provide shade, warmth (or
coolness), and protection from rain. Boots should have the right
type of sole, insulation, and ankle support.

Abide by any hunter orange requirements during the

blackpowder season. Where legal and safe, some hunters prefer to wear camouflage clothing on stand. It is still important to wear some blaze orange clothing when moving about or where hunter density is high.

Weather Considerations

You need to be prepared for the complete range of conditions possible in your hunting area. Weather can affect your comfort, safety, and mobility. If the weather changes suddenly, which it often does in hunting season, it can affect the movements of game. Short days and cool weather can trigger rutting behavior in big game, but extreme conditions can have the opposite effect. Bucks and bulls tend to be more active throughout the day when the mating urge is upon them, but heat or blizzard extremes can send them into shelter. Be prepared for the norm but also for the extreme.

Learn to anticipate the way game reacts so that you can take advantage of a change in the weather. For instance, a blizzard in the upper mountains may mean that the game will move down

Photo by Richard P. Smith   *Photo by Gerald Almy*

Knowing how game reacts to weather conditions, and being prepared for those conditions yourself, can up your odds of attaining your hunting goal.

overnight. You can prepare by being on a likely migration lane ahead of time. Remember too that the big bucks and bulls stay higher for a longer time, while does and yearlings tend to move on to lower feeding grounds.

You need to take special precautions in wet weather since even slight dampness can disable black powder. Many blackpowder hunters stretch a toy balloon over the gun's muzzle to protect it from moisture if the weather is too damp. Flintlocks are especially sensitive to wet conditions, and most hunters protect the action with a waterproof cover that they can remove in a hurry. Some don't prime the pan until ready to shoot, keeping the flash channel plugged with a small wooden peg to keep moisture out.

Caplock guns are also affected by moisture—water can seep in at the nipple or vent screw. If the powder in the breech becomes wet, pull the load, wipe the breech dry, and burn a little powder there to remove all traces of moisture. Wipe all residue from the breech before reloading.

Big Game Hunting Tactics

Several methods are employed to hunt big game, depending on the terrain, conditions, time of year, hunting pressure, the animal being hunted, and other factors. The muzzleloader hunter uses basically the same approaches as the modern-gun hunter, but must perform them more perfectly to get closer. Success often depends on the hunter's ability to choose and execute the correct tactic.

The basic hunting techniques for antlered and horned game include stand hunting, still-hunting, driving, stalking, and hunting the rut. Bears and big cats may be taken with hounds and bait.

Stand Hunting

In stand hunting, you choose the most likely spot where game will pass and remain there, still and quiet. The key to stand hunting is finding a good location, usually during scouting trips prior to hunting season. Good locations may be trail intersections, favored feeding or watering areas, rutting areas, or, when hunting pressure is heavy, escape areas.

The stand hunter may post, which is simply standing or sitting at a promising location, or he may hunt from a tree stand or blind. If the hunter is in the open, he must be very still to prevent an approaching animal from spotting him. The stand must be in a position where the approaching animal cannot scent the hunter—either downwind, crosswind, or high in a tree.

Photo by Mike Strandlund

Stand hunting from a tree or on the ground is the favored method of many blackpowder sportsmen, especially those hunting elusive game like whitetail deer.

Stand hunting is the most reliable hunting tactic for certain situations, especially for the lone hunter pursuing whitetails. The high-strung deer are very difficult to approach for a shot in their forest habitat, but their movements are fairly easy to discern from the sign they leave. Thus, it's usually better for the whitetail hunter to find a good spot and let the deer come to him.

Still-Hunting

Some hunters just don't have the patience to wait hours on stand. Or, they may have exceptional skills of stealth, or they may be hunting one of the duller-witted big game animals. For these hunters, still-hunting may be the best bet.

Still-hunting is walking very slowly through cover, stopping and remaining motionless for short periods, trying to detect animals you encounter before they detect you. This is a favorite tactic of some hunters of deer, elk, moose, and occasionally bears.

The still-hunter may hunt a certain area with a strategy in mind, or he may just walk slowly through good habitat likely to

Photo by Mike Strandlund *Photo by Richard P. Smith*

The still-hunter walks slowly and quietly, stopping frequently to examine sign and look for concealed game.

The most important element of still-hunting is moving slowly and looking hard for signs of an animal obscured behind cover, so that you see the game before it sees you.

harbor the animal he seeks. It will increase your odds considerably if you scout the area beforehand and find the pockets of game concentration where you can expect to find animals at certain times.

The still-hunter must move at a snail's pace—taking a half-hour to cover 100 yards of prime cover is not too slow. You must concentrate on trying to spot the animal before it is alarmed and dashes away. Every few steps, pause to scan the limits of your visibility. Binoculars are a great aid here. Concentrate on looking for parts of the animal—a flicking tail, a different color, or the horizontal line that indicates a belly or back.

Take great care not to make any noise and to keep the wind in your face. When you pause while hunting in woods, make your stops near a tree. You can lean on it, which makes it easier to keep still, and use it as a hiding place and shooting support. If you flush an animal, quickly analyze the situation. Hold your fire if you don't have a good chance to make a killing shot, or if there could be a person in the background.

Driving

Driving is another method of hunting cover, and can occasionally be employed in open terrain. It consists of teamwork between hunters, with drivers trying to flush animals into shooting range of standers.

Drives may be large affairs with a dozen or more hunters, or simply one hunter moving through cover toward a companion on stand. Drive hunting is viable for virtually any kind of big game, but is most used for deer and elk.

Photo by Richard P. Smith

On winter muzzleloader hunts that come after the general hunting seasons, blackpowder shooters who team up on drives often have the best success.

The most successful drives are conducted in prime habitat where there is a good concentration of game. The ideal situation is habitat where animals have predictable escape routes and can be spooked from cover with a minimum of hunters. The most common mistake among drive hunters is trying to cover too much acreage with the available hunters. Be sure to push the game in a way that it cannot scent the standers.

Keep in mind the short range of your muzzleloader. Standers should not try to cover too wide an area. Hunters taking part in drives must be especially careful in choosing their shots because of the close proximity of other hunters.

Spotting and Stalking

Spotting and stalking means glassing or scanning the landscape until game is sighted, then approaching cautiously on foot until you are within shooting distance.

To make a successful stalk, a hunter must approach the animal from downwind or crosswind, and use the topography for concealment. He must move quickly when the animal cannot see him, and freeze when it can. In some cases a hunter must move in very slow motion in order to cross an open area. He must be a master of stealth.

Difficulties the stalker may encounter include noisy ground cover, shifting breezes, and losing track of a moving animal's location. He must avoid the temptation of shooting before he is close enough.

Photo by Mike Strandlund

Spotting and stalking is the classic way of hunting big game in open mountains and prairies. The hunter glasses until he finds game, then sneaks within shooting range.

Hunting the Rut

The hunting of several big game species may coincide with their breeding season, or rut. All animals are less wary and more vulnerable to hunters during this period, and blackpowder hunters can take advantage of their lapse in caution.

Rut-hunting strategies are primarily used for male deer, elk, and moose. All three can be lured in by simulating an animal of the same species. The hunter may make a call mimicking the

Photo by Stan Warren

Animals are most suscepti-
ble when distracted and on
the move during their breeding seasons. Special tactics
such as using scents and
calling work during the rut.

Photo by Richard P. Smith

challenge of another bull or buck,
or rattle antlers and underbrush to
simulate a fight. He may also try to
convince the target animal that
there is a female that might be
ready to mate. Bugle and grunt
calls, rattling antlers, and scents are
all employed as lures.

Tracking is a difficult hunting technique to master unless the hunter is aided by
a fresh snowfall.

Hunting during the rut is productive too for the simple reason
that animals are much more on the move during daylight.

Other Big Game Hunting Methods

There are several other methods employed for big game hunting
on a smaller scale—usually variations of those mentioned above.
Some hunters seek deer, moose, caribou, or bear while silently
floating down a river. Hounds are often used to hunt bears and
mountain lions. Bait may also be used for bears, and is legal for
antlered game in some areas.

Matching Methods to the Game

Just about any of the methods mentioned above may be applied to any big game. But each must be varied somewhat for each animal, and used along with knowledge of the target animal's natural history, to give the hunter the best chance of success. Following are some approaches to taking specific big game species with a muzzleloader.

Photo by Mike Strandlund

A universal requisite in big game hunting is preventing the animal from scenting you. This hunter uses a string to monitor wind currents and positions himself so he won't be detected.

Whitetail Deer

By far the most popular big game among muzzleloader hunters is the whitetail deer. Whitetails are increasing in range and numbers; they are found in almost every state and province, and have adapted to most types of terrain, from deep woods to farmland, from plains to desert.

Whitetails are primarily nocturnal, spending daylight hours in cover and entering fields, oak groves, and other openings toward dusk to feed. They depend primarily on their sense of

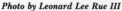

Whitetail bucks are by far the favorite target of muzzleloader hunters in America. While the deer is wary and very elusive, the typical short-range hunting conditions are conducive to hunting whitetails with muzzleloaders.

smell to detect hunters, though their hearing and ability to spot movement are also very keen. Whitetails are nervous, alert, and sneaky; they tend to move quietly, probing their surroundings with their senses. They will hide to let you pass very closely when they think you can't can see them, but can also dash and bound to safety with lightning speed.

Regardless of where or how you hunt them, whitetail deer rarely come easy. To be a successful whitetail hunter you need to weigh the odds in your favor by taking advantage of any opportunity. Opportunities can mean capitalizing on weather conditions, terrain, rutting seasons, special hunting tactics, or simply using the element of surprise. Old whitetail bucks get that way by not repeating mistakes, and successful hunters of mature whitetails take advantage of a mistake the first time the old buck makes it.

Photo by Jim Zohrer, Courtesy Wildlife Management Institute

Photo by Betty Lou Fegely

The movements of whitetails are fairly obvious by the sign they leave. Hunt them where tracks and dropping show they feed, bed, or travel.

Remember that deer are creatures of habit. Their normal schedule is to feed early and late, and to bed down during most of the day. In the hours of semidarkness, after the sun actually sets or before it rises, you are most likely to see deer. It may help to paint your front sight white in order to see it in this poor light, but be sure to check legal shooting hours and stay within them.

Pick the proper gun and load for deer. In general, states that restrict blackpowder loads set a .45-caliber minimum for deer. A better choice is .50 or larger. Most successful blackpowder hunters take whitetails at close range—under 50 yards. If possible when still-hunting and always when on stand, pick out an object— a rock or tree—at a known distance from your stand to help estimate the distance of your target.

143

Photo by Richard P. Smith

Photo by Dave Greschner

Some hunters pursuing whitetails with a muzzleloader seek a buck of trophy proportions, while others place most importance in bringing home the venison. Some areas that allow buck hunting only during the regular season permit the taking of either sex during a special muzzleloader season, which is a major attraction to some hunters.

The lone whitetail hunter generally has the best chance of success by finding a good stand and remaining there quietly. What constitutes a good stand? That depends largely on the time of year and the hunting pressure. If the muzzleloader season comes early in your area and hunting pressure is light, a stand on a field edge or open woods may be a good bet. If it is during the rut, a trail dotted with signs of buck activity is the most likely spot. If your blackpowder season attracts many hunters or if it occurs just after the regular firearms season, you're better off watching an escape route or thick hiding area where deer seek cover.

Generally, natural saddles or funnels that force deer through a narrow route from one area to another, converging game trails, and strips of cover through open areas are excellent locations for a stand.

When locating a deer stand, check prevailing winds. Cold air that collects in low spots in early morning tends to rise as the air warms during the day. This thermal movement is reversed in the evening as the air begins to cool. Weather fronts and other factors also affect wind direction. Keep these air currents in wind so the wind doesn't blow your scent toward the deer and betray your presence.

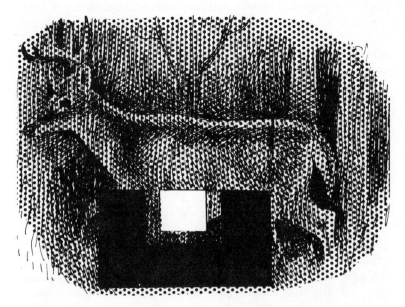

Painting your front sight white will help you get on-target in marginal light conditions, often found at dawn and dusk when whitetail hunting is best.

Photo by Lawrence Smith, Courtesy U.S. Fish and Wildlife Service

Whitetails under hunting pressure usually seek the cover of thickets and swamps. While shots here are usually well within muzzleloader range, they may be obstructed by bullet-deflecting brush.

145

While on stand, mentally rehearse what you'll do when a deer approaches. When you see a deer, move very carefully. The click made by the cocking of a hammer can instantly alarm a deer. Concealment and being completely familiar with your gun will minimize attention-getting sound and movement.

The most successful stand hunters stay seated through long hours and poor weather. Fairly poor weather of any kind has little effect on whitetails. Even in western states, whitetails are not as subject to the seasonal drift as mule deer because they stay in the willow bottoms and coulees out of natural preference for the vegetation that grows there. However, extreme wind, heat, cold, or precipitation often keeps whitetails under cover. The muzzleloader hunter can take advantage when the weather breaks and deer resume their normal activity after heavy storms or gusty winds.

Still-hunting can be productive for whitetails, especially after a rain when the woods are wet. The hunter can avoid the rhythmic footfalls that say "human" to a deer by taking a few steps and stopping, looking, and listening for the smallest indication of a nearby deer.

Don't forget binoculars. Get in the habit of stopping frequently to glass around you as you still-hunt. Deer seldom reveal themselves completely and you need to be sure you see a deer coming to prepare yourself for the shot. Using binoculars also creates movement and reflection off your hands and face that might be picked up by a deer. As a precaution, dull the shiny parts of your gear and wear dark gloves; move very slowly. Whitetails are not the sharpest-eyed animals, but they are quick to spot movement.

You'll have an advantage if the blackpowder season falls during the rut. Before the season starts, check for rubs—areas of torn up brush and skinned saplings—and scrapes, which are spots where a deer has scraped the soil bare. Bucks mark out their territories this way, and the scrapes are meeting places visited by bucks and does alike during the rut. By placing a stand near a scrape, you have a chance to catch a rutting buck unaware as he comes to investigate his "guest register."

Antler rattling is another technique the blackpowder hunter can use to attract whitetails just before and during the rut. When it hears sounds of battling bucks, a buck or doe may approach out of curiosity. Hunters may use real or simulated deer antlers to mimic the sounds of a buck fight and entice a deer to approach.

Photo by Stan Warren

If muzzleloader season coincides with the deer's peak breeding season, a whitetail hunter can be successful with calls, rattling, scent trails, and related rut-hunting tactics.

For best results, rattling should be accompanied by the realistic sounds of thrashing brush and pounding turf. This method is recommended only for areas where hunter density is sparse and the rattler displays blaze orange in full view.

As hunters have learned more and more about how vocal whitetails actually are, the prospect of calling deer has opened a new range of opportunities for the blackpowder hunter. Deer respond to the imitation of grunts and bleats by other deer, and will sometimes approach to within range of a muzzleloader.

The dates of the whitetail rut vary with latitude and other factors. Northern hunters find rutting bucks in early fall, while the rut may last into springtime in the southern or desert zones. The vast majority of whitetail rut activity is in the middle of November. Many states' muzzleloader seasons precede the regular gun season, and this can place the blackpowder hunter in the peak of rutting season and improve his chances of getting a deer.

When put on full-alert by hunting pressure, whitetail bucks become very hard to hunt one-on-one. If there are many hunters in the woods, take advantage of them and let them push the deer to you. Get into the woods early, far off a road near likely escape cover. While other hunters walk, keep still on stand. Or get together with some friends to organize some drives. Pick out some smaller woodlots and creekbottoms to keep the drive to manageable size. Put standers in areas where deer are likely to try to sneak out, rather than run for it. They'll be much easier to take with a one-shot rifle.

Usually encountered in thick cover at close range, the whitetail is an excellent target for the hunter with a close- range gun. The combination of availability, challenging hunting, and delicious meat make whitetail deer by far the most popular game for the muzzleloader hunter. For more whitetail hunting information, see the NRA Hunter Skills Series book, *Whitetail Deer Hunting*.

Mule Deer

Mule deer and their subspecies, blacktail and Sitka deer, live throughout western North America. Muleys behave quite differently from whitetails and tend to live in more open terrain. You'll generally see mule deer much farther away than you would see a whitetail, and as a muzzleloader hunter, you'll be tempted to take longer shots at muleys. Keep your effective shooting range in mind, however, and remember that it is easier to get closer to a muley.

Photo by Jim Zumbo

Mule deer inhabit the mountains, plains, desert, and coastal forests of the American West. Though they're considered less wary than whitetails, a mule deer buck like this is very hard to collect with a short-range firearm.

Mule deer are found in small herds throughout the year and bucks tend to remain in loose bachelor groups well into the fall. Like whitetails, mule deer are more active during hunting hours during the rut. Otherwise, morning and evening are peak activity periods. Mule deer like to bed near the top of a small hill or gully where they have a good view while they rest, yet are able to drop out of sight if alarmed. Mule deer have excellent hearing and eyesight, and scan their surroundings for any source of sound or movement.

In the mountains, mule deer migrate seasonally. Deep snow can bring them down to much lower elevations; they may be here today and gone tomorrow. Muzzleloader seasons for mule deer usually occur in these transitional seasons—from mid September to late October. Prepare for your hunt to be one of extremes.

Most blackpowder hunters seeking mule deer take a stand, still-hunt, or combine those methods. Spotting and stalking is the best tactic in some areas, particularly the largely open habitat of sagebrush, pinyon, and juniper that covers much of the West.

In stand hunting, pick a location such as a watering area, the head of a draw, bottom of a ravine, or some other travel route

149

Photo by Rex Thomas

Big muley bucks tend to favor rugged high country until deep snow forces them into lower elevations. Hunting here requires exhausting hikes and long stalks.

with well-used game trails. Two-man drives through small pockets of cover often trick muleys into the lap of a companion hunter. Another good tactic is to combine driving and still-hunting. You and your partner can still-hunt parallel to one another on a slope or on either side of a ridge; you may walk up on a deer, or spook it to your friend.

Winds can be unpredictable in mountains and high plains country, so plan your stalking and still-hunting with wind direction in mind. Learn the wind drift characteristics of your hunting loads. The mule deer rutting season can give the muzzleloader hunter an advantage. Like whitetails, mule deer preoccupied with breeding move more and are less wary.

The mating period for mule deer varies according to region. Keep this in mind when planning your hunt. In general, big bucks tend to stay higher in the mountains and most hunters in the Rockies tend to get their big bucks around timberline. During breeding time, however, they will descend to lower elevations where the most does are. Wildlife managers and hunters who monitor mule deer can tell you when the rut is at its peak.

You'll find that many big muley bucks can be as cagey as whitetails, and will often stay hidden rather than break cover as young bucks and does are more likely to do. The big boys tend to hang out among sagebrush or juniper where they can watch for approaching predators. In more open plains country, look

150

Photo by Jim Zumbo

Photo by Rex Thomas

Mule deer depend heavily on keen eyesight, and in open country are difficult to approach. Successful hunters usually take their deer by spotting and stalking, though still-hunting, driving patches of cover, and other methods produce.

for bucks at the heads of small hills or draws that offer them the best chances of escape.

The hunter seeing a trophy mule deer buck for the first time after becoming accustomed to whitetails is struck by the much larger antlers. A mule deer's antlers can best be judged by comparing the length of the ears to the size of the rack. Headgear on a trophy muley extends well beyond the ears in width, and sweeps upward to twice as high as ear length.

Keep in mind that blackpowder seasons for mule deer sometimes fall at the same time or in combination with elk and bear seasons. This is an excellent opportunity for the muzzleloader hunter to pursue multiple species. Check all regulations for the management area you plan to hunt.

Pronghorn

While the pronghorn is often considered long-range game for flat-shooting centerfire loads, it is a popular target for muzzleloader hunters with advanced shooting or stalking abilities. Stealth, planning, and patience are key ingredients for a successful pronghorn muzzleloader hunt.

Hunting the pronghorn, or antelope, is a special challenge with a blackpowder firearm. A pronghorn's eyesight has been compared to an eight-power scope. The blackpowder hunter can even the score by taking along binoculars.

Compared to deer, pronghorns in their open country habitat aren't hard to spot. The problem is getting within shooting range,

Photo by Richard P. Smith

The pronghorn is generally considered a long-range target, but a good stalk or ambush near a waterhole can get a muzzleloader hunter within range of the prairie speedster.

which in most cases involves stalking. The sparse cover typical in antelope country means that you'll have to plan your approach carefully. The last few yards getting into muzzleloader range are the most crucial.

Pronghorns live in flat, featureless country as a defense; they depend on their eyesight to spot predators and their swiftness to escape. Some pronghorns are simply unapproachable; in other cases, you'll be forced to take advantage of slight breaks in the topography to stay hidden.

Many hunters pursue the pronghorn by spotting it first from a vehicle, then hiding the rig and beginning a stalk. Other hunters prefer to head out across the plains into roadless areas, glassing the horizon for signs of a herd. If you spot a huntable antelope near a break in the landscape, such as a tight basin, wash, or narrow valley, move in quickly until you approach the highest point; then drop to your belly and crawl. You might peek over the ridgeline and find your trophy standing within muzzleloader shooting distance, or he might be gone. Invest in some elbow and knee pads to take the pain out of contact with the rocks and cactus that appear only when you are trying to crawl through ankle-high grass.

Photo by Jeff Murray

Because shots at pronghorn are often taken near a blackpowder hunter's maximum range, he must be skilled with his gun and a good judge of range in open country.

Pronghorns can see white for a long distance, and are curious, which has led to development of a hunting tactic. Tie a white rag to a stick and raise it above your head while you hide behind a bluff or some other landform. This can occasionally lure a pronghorn into shooting range, appealing to the animal's curiosity. Pronghorns can also be attracted with a pronghorn decoy, or even with a predator call designed for fox or coyote.

Another technique is to hide behind a lightweight camouflage shield while you approach the antelope. If such a strategy is impossible, set up a stand at a waterhole or fence crossing. Antelope are not good jumpers and will tend to go around or under a fence at the same spot. Such crossings can serve as a blind or an ambush site. Stands near watering areas can be equally productive if you take special care to hide yourself.

The pronghorn is comparatively small and easy to bring down, weighing about 100 pounds. The gun and its shooter should be accurate at longer ranges. Wind and bullet drift can be crucial considerations in open prairies because of the animal's relatively small size and limited vital zone.

One advantage in hunting the antelope is that its vital zone is conveniently marked. The white markings of its belly and sides meet with the tan "saddle" in a line just above the elbow, marking the vertical line of the "crosshairs" at the vital spot.

In hunting pronghorn with a muzzleloader, be very careful in estimating yardage. In open country, animals usually appear closer than they really are. Also, avoid trying running shots that might tempt a hunter with a modern rifle. Your chief tactic will be stealth and skill to get within accurate shooting range.

Trophy hunters usually find the biggest bucks with horns of 13 inches or better in the most remote portions of their terrain.

Photo by Jim Zumbo

The biggest antelope bucks—those with horns of 13 inches and longer—are usually found far from roads in the most remote parts of their habitat.

Elk

Once inhabiting most of the continent, elk were decimated during the westward expansion. Conservation efforts have been successful, however, and elk now roam timbered mountainsides throughout the West. They have also been transplanted to a few other areas where they are sometimes hunted. The prospect of a challenging hunt, impressive antlers, and delicious meat make elk hunting a favorite form of western big game hunting.

155

USDA-Soil Conservation Service Photo

Elk hunting has become increasingly popular among blackpowder hunters. Mature bulls carry awesome antlers and an ample amount of delicious meat.

Using a muzzleloader for elk not only gives the hunter an extra element of interest; it can actually be an advantage. Blackpowder elk seasons often occur before the general season, when more animals are available and they have not yet been spooked by hunters. Sometimes muzzleloader hunting coincides with the rut, when animals are more active and less wary. There are often limited entry units or cow permits that the muzzleloader can obtain.

Elk are among our biggest big game, with large bulls over five feet high at the shoulder weighing 800 or more pounds. Elk prefer to walk, but can sustain a trot of 25 miles per hour all day and for short periods can gallop at 35 to 40.

While deer are browsers, feeding mainly on buds and twigs, elk are primarily grazers, feeding on grasses. Many hunters know this and take stands on the edges of meadows. However, elk today are very wary and spend most daylight hours in dark timber. Elk are much more shade-oriented than deer. Whereas mule deer will commonly linger in the open for some time after sunrise before bedding, elk want to be back in the timber at first light. They'll stay in dark forests all day, and won't head out to feed until it's almost night. If grass grows in the timber, they may not come out to feed at all, preferring to remain in the forest.

Winter snows force elk to lower elevations where forage is available. Migrations are a fact of life for elk; they generally use

National Park Service Photo

Muzzleloader hunters have a distinct advantage when the elk season coincides with bugling time. Bulls divulge their locations and sometimes come to bugling and cow calling.

the same routes to migrate each year. During breeding season bulls gather harems of cows, challenging each other for as many cows as they can round up. The breeding period occurs chiefly in September, running into early October. The peak of the rut is usually from mid to late September.

During the rut, bulls spend most of their time guarding cows, breeding them, and chasing off intruding bulls. Typically, a herd bull will control a half dozen or so cows, occasionally over a dozen.

After the rut, elk vocalization and competition diminishes. They gather in larger groups, and by the time winter sets in, bulls are often joined together in herds numbering as many as 20 or more.

Because elk live in herds, much of the range will be barren of elk, so they're difficult to locate. Disturbed elk normally head for the most remote, rugged country they can find. There is practically no blowdown or thicket too dense for elk. For that reason, hunters must work hard to locate animals. It's usually necessary to walk, hike, and climb several miles a day to effectively cover elk country.

Hunters fail at elk hunting primarily because they're unwilling to penetrate the forests to hunt elk. Too many hunters wait in

157

vain, hoping to spot animals in clearings. That tactic might work well in wilderness areas or units where hunter pressure is light, but is seldom successful where elk are disturbed.

Elk can cover large areas of forested wilderness. Bedding and watering areas can be miles apart. A herd leaves a large amount of sign but solitary bulls before the rut are hard to find. You can find elk herds by droppings and tracks, by sightings, and by hearing the bugles of bulls during the rut.

Sometimes you can learn an elk's daily routine. The very early morning is usually spent feeding unless the elk are disturbed, when they may feed only at night. Otherwise look for them in jackpine thickets in flat country and in dense areas that provide shade and security in mountains. Travel lanes between feeding and breeding areas are excellent places to set up.

Many muzzleloader seasons for elk coincide with the September rut. As the bulls come down to join the herds of cow elk, they may be called in by imitating their bugling. In recent years, with bugling becoming very popular among hunters, bull elk tend not to respond as readily to man-made bugles. The chirp and other sounds made by cow elk can be used to attract bulls. Calling is becoming increasingly sophisticated as hunters learn more about elk habits and vocalizations.

Bull elk during rut make rubs and mud wallows. You can smell these wallows as easily as you can see them. The strong odor comes from the bull elk's urine, which he sprays on himself

Photo by Stan Warren

and in the wallows he makes. A rutting bull also tears up brush, trees, and ground with his antlers and hooves. It is not unusual to see bulls in rut caked with mud, with branches and other debris caught in their antlers.

Effective elk hunting tactics include calling, stalking, still-hunting, driving, and stand hunting.

Bugle occasionally as you hunt through an area to help locate a solitary bull. Be aware of wind direction and use available cover to screen your movement. If a bull returns your bugle call, you may thrash trees, make a cow call, and try other strategy to urge him in. If you spot him coming your way, and he is not likely to scent you or become hidden in brush, hold your fire. Don't make the mistake of shooting too soon.

Stalking and still-hunting are also effective tactics for some blackpowder elk hunters. A hunter who has some prime mountain parks located may get there before first light and watch for elk wrapping up their nightly feeding. The hunter may stalk the elk in the park, or calculate where the elk will re-enter the timber and try to intercept them.

Still-hunting may be a good method where the hunter knows likely bedding areas of elk. Creeping very slowly into the wind, a skillful still-hunter can sneak well within shooting range of bedded elk.

In areas of near-barren mountains with small pockets of timber, driving elk works well. Hunters must be careful not to take running shots that are more likely to wound than kill.

For the best shot possible, get close and be thoroughly familiar with how your gun will shoot at different ranges. The point of aim should be just below the mid line of the elk's body and

Photo by Stan Warren

The most difficult part of elk hunting is getting in and out of back-country that has good numbers of game. Outfitters and packstrings are often necessary for the best shot as a successful elk hunt.

behind the front shoulder. Try to avoid anything but a two- lung shot.

Plan your hunt early, since many elk hunting states have non-resident application deadlines as early as January or February of the year of the hunt. This planning will pay off because many states have a combination deer and elk license, ideal for the blackpowder hunter.

Because of the elk's great size and strength, you should use at least a .54-caliber rifle, work up a potent hunting load, and restrict your shooting range.

Moose

The moose is excellent game for the blackpowder hunter to pursue, because he is approachable to the close range required for a muzzleloader. But his mass dictates a potent load and well-placed shot. The largest antlered big game animals in the world, moose weigh up to 1,800 pounds.

Photo by Gabby Barrus

The moose is the largest animal receiving any appreciable attention from muzzleloader hunters. Moose can often be approached closely, but the shot must still be a potent load placed precisely.

Moose are northern forest animals that spend most of their time close to waterways and wetlands. The Alaska-Yukon moose is the largest. The Wyoming moose, found also in Montana, parts of Utah, Colorado, Idaho, and neighboring areas, is the smallest. The Canada moose is most common, found in all provinces and also in Maine, Minnesota, and other northern states.

How you hunt moose with black powder will depend on the

terrain. In most of their range, moose prefer willow and alder thickets close to water. In most of eastern Canada, the flat country and dense cover generally require approaching by canoe, provided hunting season occurs before freeze-up. Check the shoreline for moose sign; early and late in the day are best. If you spot a moose ahead of time in an area, chances are he'll stick around until you come hunting for him, since moose are not the wanderers elk or deer are.

A good pair of field glasses will help you find moose at a distance. The big animals aren't particularly perceptive or wary, and may be approached to within shooting range in waist-high brush.

Western moose are generally hunted backpack-style or on horseback. In the East, stand hunting works better because prime moose habitat is more abundant and the animals are less likely to wander from their home territory.

Stalking can be effective if you remember that a moose's main defense is its sense of smell. Keep the wind in your face and if cover is absent, move in on the moose while its head is down.

If you hunt moose in snow, still-hunting may work best. Follow a moose trail or walk through an area that contains fresh sign, pausing every few steps to watch and listen, heading into the wind. When you spot the moose, get close and pick your shot carefully.

Another technique that works during the rutting season—usually in mid-September—is imitating the mating call of the cow moose. Find where moose are feeding on the edge of a lake. Use an Indian-style birchbark megaphone or your cupped hands to project your imitation of the mating grunt of a cow moose. Pour water from the call into the lake, simulating the sound of a cow moose urinating.

Moose should be hunted with at least a .54-caliber muzzleloader. Get close and pick a heart, lung, or neck shot.

Don't shoot a moose that is standing belly-deep in water; getting it ashore to field dress can be very difficult. Any hunter who has field dressed one will agree there is no such thing as a small moose. If you're successful, you'll have a half-ton of choice meat. To manage it, have along a small block and tackle and plenty of rope, in addition to an extra pack frame.

Caribou

Caribou herds roam the vast wilderness of Canada and Alaska and can be hunted in subarctic tundra, northern forests, and

Photo by Russ Carpenter

Caribou is an excellent quarry for the muzzleloader hunter. The animals are normally plentiful, can be encountered at close range, and seem to fall easiy to a well-placed shot.

high mountains above timberline. Five subspecies are recognized in North America, with more in northern Europe and Asia.

Caribou bulls of the larger subspecies average 500 pounds, while those of the smaller breeds weigh about 325. Unlike any other members of the North American deer family, both males and females sport antlers. The antlers of mature bulls are sweeping, dramatic trophies. Caribou are always on the move, usually traveling in herds, especially in spring and fall migration.

Caribou, like moose, may be approached rather easily for a close-range muzzleloader shot. The problem is locating them in the first place. Caribou can be plentiful or absent. Prepare for a lot of walking or riding and glassing.

In mountainous country, look for caribou by glassing the high slopes. In this open habitat, caribou aren't hard to spot. The next problem is getting into blackpowder range. Plan a careful stalk. A band of caribou is constantly moving and their habitat offers very little cover, so concealing yourself can be difficult. Caribou change directions on a whim and can end up anywhere but where you expect them to be. Be quiet and move carefully, into the wind as much as possible. Not known for its intelligence, a spooked caribou will sometimes come back to see what scared it and give you a second chance. For the last hundred yards, be sure you are wearing your crawling clothes.

The caribou hunter should carry at least a .50-caliber rifle. A .54 will be better if you also plan to hunt other big game in caribou country such as sheep, moose, or bear.

If you hunt before the caribou rut you'll have a better chance of bringing home good meat. At the onset of the rut, the meat of a bull caribou becomes tough and strong-tasting. During the early season, most caribou have antlers still in velvet. This won't harm the trophy. You may leave the velvet on, or scrape it off with a knife.

Black Bear and Mountain Lion

Black bear and mountain lions are popular targets for muzzleloader hunters because shots are usually at close range. A well-placed first shot is especially important when face-to-face with these dangerous predators, and a backup firearm is recommended.

Black bear live throughout the United States, Canada, and Alaska, and a good bear hunt is generally within reasonable traveling distance of the average blackpowder hunter. Depending on where you hunt, you can expect to encounter mature bears weighing 150 pounds, or 500 pounds and more. In some regions, especially the Rocky Mountain states, the "black" bear may have a coat of light brown or even blond. Mountain lions live throughout western North America.

Photo by Gabby Barrus   *Photo by Len Rue Jr.*

Black bear and cougar are popular among muzzleloader hunters because they offer close targets when hunted correctly.

There are several methods of hunting bears. They may be stalked, driven, and still-hunted in the way antlered game is hunted, but most bear hunters use dogs or bait.

Most popular in many areas is hunting over bait. Hunting seasons may be in the spring or fall, but bears are particularly attracted to bait in spring after they wake from their winter sleep and are especially hungry. Because their fur is prime at this time, they make excellent trophies. Depending on local regulations, bait can be anything from a dead horse, a winter-killed deer, a bucket of rough fish, or even a pile of logs covered with molasses or jam.

Blackpowder guns are well-suited to baited bear hunts because you will be in a blind or tree stand, and will usually have a close target and plenty of time to prepare for your shot. One drawback is that the light may be very poor at the time the bear comes to the bait—early or late in the day. For this reason, you can extend your shooting time a bit by painting your front sight white for better visibility. A second drawback is that a spring bear hunt in

Photo by Stan Warren

Photo by Rex Thomas

A bear gun should be at least .50 caliber if the hunter stalks or hunts over bait, while a muzzleloader used to de-tree a cougar can be as light as .40 caliber.

the north country will find you at the onset of the prime season for blackflies and other blood-sucking insects, when hunters discover bug protection is more important than their gun.

In hunting over bait with a muzzleloader, the position of your stand is important. It should be downwind or crosswind of the bear's probable direction of approach to keep him from scenting you. It should offer a clear lane and a good angle for shooting. You'll need to be motionless for long periods, so take some kind of ground cover to protect yourself from cold and dampness. Place a cushion between you and the tree or rock you'll be leaning against. A poncho, preferably in camouflage, will shield you and your gun from a shower.

Hunting with the aid of hounds is productive for both bears and mountain lions. In most cases, due to the expense of keeping and training packs of hounds for hunting, the muzzleloader hunter generally hires the services of a guide for this kind of hunt. Hound hunting requires you to be in excellent physical shape, because it means following after the hounds until they have the bear or lion cornered or treed. While a bear or lion may look calmly down from the upper tree branches, allowing the hunter to approach and choose his shot, sometimes they make a break or charge into the midst of dogs and hunters. The hunt at this point becomes frantic and exciting.

For bears over bait or in a tree, a .50 caliber loaded with a conical is sufficient. If there's a chance you could be taking longer shots at bears, go to a .54. Most hunters use small calibers for treed cougars, as small as a .36 caliber if backup guns are present.

Boar and Javelina
Wild hogs offer an exciting challenge for the blackpowder hunter. In some states wild hogs are increasing and are considered the property of the landowner; they may be hunted any time of year with his permission, without a license. In other states wild hogs are rare, but the imported European or "Russian" boar can be found in limited huntable numbers. For the most part, hogs that are hunted are feral—free-roaming descendants from domestic stock that went wild. Prime hog states are Georgia, Florida, Tennessee, Mississippi, Alabama, Louisiana, Arkansas, Texas, and California.

In general, the color and size of these animals depends on the stock from which they originated. Generally regarded as detrimental to farm crops, timber, and other wildlife, hogs are fun

Photos by Rex Thomas

Hog hunting is gaining popularity as wild hogs increase in numbers. They can often be stalked closely for a sure, single shot.

to hunt. Once you locate a group of hogs, they are fairly easy to stalk if you keep the wind right.

A boar hog gone wild can weigh well over 400 pounds, though most weigh less than half that. A .54-caliber firearm won't be too much, since the thick hide of the hog can be hard to penetrate, particularly around the neck and shoulders.

Hogs spend the daylight hours in cool shade with lots of cover, and range mostly during the hours of dusk and dawn. They also tend move about and rest in groups. Their rooting behavior makes them easier to trail than most big game. Hog tracks, though similar in size to a whitetail's, can be distinguished by their more curved shape.

Javelina are small, pig-like animals found in the high deserts of Texas, Arizona, and New Mexico. They aren't much bigger than a coyote but look and act like wild hogs. Like pigs they are social, hide out during the heat of the day, and forage at night for prickly pear cactus, pine nuts, or whatever they find. A few hunters use dogs to hunt javelina, but the blackpowder hunter can use the still-hunting method, watching for groups moving in and out of draws. A stalk is generally required to get within range. A .45-caliber rifle is ideal for javelina.

A javelina has long, bristly hair, particularly along its back. This makes the animal look bigger than it is and can mislead you when you pick your shot. A well-placed blackpowder shot is near what looks like the center of the body behind the distinctive neck band that gives the animal its other name, collared peccary. A carefully placed shot in the ribs is the best. Avoid head shots if you want to save the trophy. Javelina meat is delicious, but get the hide off as soon as you can, and take care to cut deeply around the scent gland at the base of the hips in the middle of the back to keep it from tainting the meat.

After the Shot

Ideally, you have stalked your game to very close quarters, have a clear shot, good angle, and steady aim. Your shot pierces the heart, both lungs, or upper spine, and the animal drops quickly within sight.

This ideal situation is not always the case, however. Often a

Photo by Richard P. Smith

Trailing game after the shot is a skill every hunter should master. Learn to look at clues such as hair swatches and track characteristics at times when the blood trail is thin.

hunter must trail his quarry before he finds and recovers it. Sometimes the trail is a difficult one to follow. There are procedures that can make it easier.

When you shoot, pay close attention to how and where the animal runs. This is especially difficult in muzzleloader hunting, because the animal will likely be obscured in a cloud of white smoke. But try hard to note the point where the animal vanishes as it dashes away. Reload your rifle, and find the blood trail. If it is faint, mark the blood spots as you follow so you can backtrack if you lose the trail.

When you find the animal, ascertain if it is alive or dead. If it is lying on its side with its eyes open and unblinking, it is dead. If its head is up or eyes are closed, approach cautiously and dispatch it with a precise, close-range shot to the head, neck, or heart.

Field dress the animal quickly, beginning with a cut from anus to brisket. Extend the cut through the breastbone and well into the throat if you have the proper cutting tools and do not wish to save the cape. Pull out the intestines, cutting connective tissue

Photo by Richard P. Smith

After locating your downed animal, follow the correct procedure. Usually they must be tagged immediately, then field dressed, and packed out whole or in quarters.

Photo by Stan Warren

Photo by Jim Zumbo

free where necessary, being sure to remove the heart, lungs, and windpipe from above the diaphragm muscle. Remove the genitals, and cut out the rectum and anus. Wipe out the body cavity and open it to let air circulate, but cover it with cloth if flies are present. In warm weather, skin the animal and cool the meat quickly to preserve its flavor.

Smaller big game like deer and antelope are usually transported from the field whole, either by manual dragging, pack animal, or some kind of cart or vehicle. Larger animals must be quartered or deboned and taken out in pieces.

After-the-shot procedures are outlined in more detail in other NRA Hunter Skills Series books such as *Western Big Game Hunting.*

Big Game Trophies

In big game hunting, a trophy is in the eyes of the beholder. Each hunter has his own idea of what constitutes a big game trophy.

If you want to have a neck or shoulder mount made, your animal must be properly caped, which means skinning the head, neck, and shoulders so that the cuts are not apparent in the finished mount. This process requires care, or the cape will be ruined.

Photo by Mike Strandlund

Many big game animals make a beautiful, fascinating trophy when mounted. Knowing you took it with a single-shot, short-range gun makes the souvenir even more satisfying.

Take proper precautions as you field dress the animal. When making the incision to remove the entrails, stop at the brisket if you want a shoulder mount. Never cut the animal's throat to bleed it or cut away the windpipe.

Before caping, photograph the head from different positions. This will help the taxidermist later when he mounts your animal.

To cape, start by cutting completely around the body ahead of the ribcage. At the top of the back, make a straight cut toward the back of the head. Stop between the antlers and make a cut to each antler, using a screwdriver to push the hide away from the antler burrs, cutting as you go. Next, cut from the brisket down to the foreleg at each knee. Keep cutting, pulling the hide toward the head inside out as you would a sock. Carefully free the hide from the face, being careful to include the eyelashes, ears, and nose. If you don't feel competent doing this, skin just the neck and shoulders, cutting the head off under the chin. Your taxidermist will do the rest.

Salt the hide immediately, or quick-freeze it if you can't deliver it to a taxidermist right away. Don't fail to salt it if it isn't frozen. Hair will slip after just a day or two. Don't spare the salt. Use at least a pound for a deer-size animal, two or more for a moose or elk cape.

Big Game Trophy Programs

Besides the Boone and Crockett Club and Safari Club International big game trophy recognition programs, there are several special programs for exceptional trophies taken by hunters with muzzleloaders.

The National Muzzle Loading Rifle Association oversees the Longhunter Society, and maintains this big game trophy program and a recordbook for trophies taken with a muzzleloader. For more information, contact The Longhunter Society, PO Box 67, Friendship, IN 47021 or call (812) 667-5131.

The National Rifle Association of America awards plaques to muzzleloader hunters for taking trophy animals that meet minimum standards. Muzzleloader hunters are also eligible to enter the NRA Leatherstocking Award Contest. This award is presented annually to the hunter taking the highest-ranked trophy. For more information on the program, write to the National Rifle Association of America, Hunter Services Division, 1600 Rhode Island Ave. NW, Washington, DC 20036 or telephone (202) 828-6240.

CHAPTER 8
SMALL GAME AND WATERFOWL HUNTING

Blackpowder hunting for small game is a quaint mix of peaceful relaxation and thrilling challenge. It may be a leisurely stroll where the bushytails thrive, persuasive tolling at the edge of the duck pond, or tactical maneuvers in the turkey woods. It is slower paced than the small game hunting most of us are familiar with, rewarding the hunter for patience and skill.

Photo by Bob Belford

Black powder adds an element of interest and challenge in gunning for small game and waterfowl.

Considering the time and commotion required to reload a muzzleloader in the field, the value of a single, well-placed shot is very apparent. The key to success for the small game hunter is to set up that well-placed shot. There are a number of factors to consider in planning a hunt, and failure to consider any one of them can make the difference between a successful hunt and disappointment.

The Small Game Blackpowder Gun

Start by choosing a firearm appropriate to the game being sought. The most popular for small game and birds is the shot-

Photos by Mike Strandlund

The type of animal and way you pursue it will determine your choice of blackpowder firearm.

gun. A shotgun offers a wide range of projectile sizes and shot patterns, making it adaptable to nearly any need. Guidelines for tailoring the shotgun load for different kinds of birds and small game are found in Chapter 6. In general, the smaller the animal being hunted, the smaller the shot size or caliber rifle that will be used. Smaller, faster game require a smaller pellet size that puts a larger number of projectiles into a wider shot pattern. Larger game requires a larger pellet size with greater energy to assure a clean harvest. Always a balance is sought between making a quick, clean harvest and preserving a maximum of usable meat or hide.

Some small game hunters prefer to use a rifle with a single projectile. A rifle of any caliber—even a big game rifle—can be used for head shots on squirrels or rabbits without damaging meat. The traditional rifle calibers for small game are .32 and .36. For the larger members of the small game community, such as coyotes, .45 caliber may be more appropriate.

An Approach to Small Game Hunting

Game animals from mourning doves to bobcats have some things in common. They all need food, they all drink water, and they all must rest in shelter. Knowledge of the game animal sought will help you determine what is good habitat for that animal. Some animals require open bodies of water; most prefer to live in habitat dominated by certain vegetation. South-facing slopes give warmth on chilly mornings, while north slopes provide shady shelter from noonday heat. Some animals want long vistas so they can see open areas on all sides. Some like hidden little nooks and crannies. Everything the hunter knows about the quarry will help in evaluating whether a piece of property has the qualities of good living for that game animal.

Once landowner permission has been obtained, the terrain can be sized up more closely. The banks of streams, the edges of ponds, even the mud around a rain puddle may show signs of game. Look for tracks, droppings, and bits of fur or dropped feathers. These may also be good clues to an area being used by animals for dust baths or by birds for graveling. Nibbled plants, nut or seed hulls, feathers or fur, gnawed bones, and discarded corn cobs are valuable clues in identifying feeding sites.

Most animals have a favorite kind of cover where they feel

safe and well-hidden. Rabbits, for instance, favor brush piles while doves often like a stand of evergreen trees. Trails can often be identified by a careful observer, and experience and practice will make them easier to find.

Photo by Mike Strandlund   *Photo by Dwain Bland*

Good habitat—especially the availability of food—is the key to good small game populations. The smart hunter knows what to look for and scouts out the prime areas.

Generalizations about a particular game species are a good place to start, but local conditions can change the game habits and affect the actual hunt. Experienced hunters in the area can be a good source of information, but nothing can substitute for personal knowledge of a particular environment. Time in the field actually observing game, listening, and developing game awareness is the best way to learn. A practiced hunter never stops looking for signs of game.

Limitations of the hunter, as well as the limitations of muzzleloading guns, will affect decisions about where and how to hunt. In shooting flying birds, the slower ignition of the blackpowder charge and the longer reloading time make pass shooting at birds that are traveling by less productive than hunting over a place where birds are setting in. Scouting out areas where birds are feeding, where they come to rest at evening, or where they come to hide when pressured may pay off very well. Many birds can also be lured with decoys and calls to attempt landings nearby. As the game comes in, the wise hunter remembers the lower velocity of the muzzleloading firearm's charge and the limits of the gun's reach and pattern.

The best way to hunt many types of small game, as well as big game, is stand hunting. In stand-hunting, staying undetected is the key factor. The most important part of visual concealment is motion control. Suppressing unnecessary movement and reducing the amount of motion needed to observe the area and get off the shot are priorities in staying hidden.

Photo by Rex Thomas

Camouflage is most important when hunting keen-eyed, sharp-witted game like coyotes and turkeys.

Some game animals, like upland birds, are more successfully hunted by pursuit than by waiting. It is helpful to have a trained dog along for this kind of action. For muzzleloading hunters, a bird dog that will point and hold is usually more effective than a dog that will flush birds. The shorter reach of the blackpowder shotgun can make a dog that ranges away from the hunter of very little value.

Wild Turkeys

The wild turkey is an increasingly popular target for the muzzleloading hunter. It's a traditional target, a favorite of pioneers, the original blackpowder hunters. Turkey populations are growing across the country, offering increased hunting opportunities and chances of success.

Photo by Rick Hacker

Photo by F.R. Martin

Turkey hunting requires skillful tactics and good loads. Experts agree that turkeys are among the most challenging gamebirds to hunt and toughest birds to kill.

There is evidence that turkeys in early times were not as wary as today. Traditional methods of hunting were stalking and bagging turkeys with a shotgun, sniping them at longer range with rifles, and shooting them from their roost in morning and evening.

Today hunting ethics, laws, and safety concerns prohibit these traditional methods. Hunting regulations often prohibit shooting turkeys with rifles and hunting in the evening. The combination of camouflage and larger numbers of hunters in the woods preclude stalking or still-hunting for the birds, because of the safety risks of these methods.

The standard turkey hunting method today is to call birds into shotgun range or, where legal, take them with a rifle from a stand.

Turkeys are the biggest game birds in America, with gobblers averaging around 20 pounds. Shotgun loads should be close to the maximum safe load. In blackpowder shotguns the 12-gauge is acceptable, but the 10 is recommended. With a heavy charge of 4 or 6 shot and a tight pattern from a full-choke, standing turkeys may be taken with a head shot up to 40 yards away. To test the performance of your gun and load, pattern shots at various distances on a lifesize outline of the head and neck of a turkey. You should be able to hit the outline with a minimum of six pellets with each shot. If you can't, you must shorten your shooting range or improve your load.

If your shotgun has open chokes, you will probably have to call the turkey to 20 yards or less for an effective killing shot. Never try to take a turkey with a shot to the body unless you are very close and have heavy loads of large pellets.

Guns of .36 or .45 caliber sighted-in precisely are the best muzzleloading rifles for turkeys. Riflemen should aim for the turkey's wing butt; hitting the head is too difficult, and a shot in the breast will ruin most of the meat. The gobbler's wing butt vital zone is about the size of a tennis ball; it is smaller on a hen.

Photo by Dwain Bland

A rifle used for turkey hunting must be capable of placing shots into the turkey's baseball-size vital zone near the wing butt under field conditions. Rifles are illegal for turkey hunting in some areas.

The most popular turkey hunting method is luring gobblers to close range during the spring mating season. The hunter first locates a tom, usually by hearing a gobble. He may locate the bird in the evening as it goes to its roost, returning to hunt in the morning, or he may hear a bird during the morning and sneak into calling range. Then he sets up, as camouflaged as possible without restricting his ability to get a shot, and uses one of many types of calling devices to begin calling. He simulates the clucks, yelps, and other calls made by the hen turkey. Ideally, the gobbler approaches into shooting range.

During fall seasons hens, gobblers, and young of the year are usually open game. Many turkeys are taken by riflemen on deer stands. Shotgunners may hunt turkeys by locating a flock, sneaking close, scaring the birds into scattering, then calling one back. It is seldom possible to get a shot on the scatter, because it is very difficult to get within the necessary 20-30 yard range.

Hunters occasionally take turkeys by waiting on stand. Good stand locations are favored fall feeding areas, dusting areas, and strutting grounds—open areas where gobblers strut and display in the springtime breeding ritual.

Turkeys are very wary and have extremely good eyesight and hearing. Prospective turkey hunters must read up on the birds' habits and hunting tactics, and practice calling, shooting, and use of camouflage.

Detailed information on turkey hunting can be found in the NRA Hunter Skills Series book, *Wild Turkey Hunting*, available from NRA Hunter Services Division.

Waterfowl

Waterfowl hunting is among the most challenging pursuits of the blackpowder shooter. Ducks and geese are often big in body

Photos by Mike Strandlund

The tough feathers and fast, high flight of waterfowl make them difficult targets for the blackpowder shotgunner.

with heavy feathers and bones protecting vital areas. Their fast flight makes them elusive targets, and the flocking tendency leads to situations where the shooter will miss opportunities because his one or two shots are expended. Waterfowling is often best in rain and snow, which play havoc with the performance of the muzzleloading shotgun.

Blackpowder waterfowl shotguns should be choked 10 or 12 gauges charged with heavy loads. Traditional shotgun loads for waterfowl were No. 6 lead shot for small ducks like teal, 4s for larger ducks like mallards, and 2s for geese. These waterfowl loads are now outlawed in most areas, and will be obsolete as of the 1991 hunting season, due to federally mandated use of steel shot for waterfowl hunters. Muzzleloader hunters will need shotguns designed to shoot steel shot without being damaged, and move up to No. 4, No. 2, and BB to replace the sizes mentioned above. Again, the guns and loads should be pattern-tested to determine load performance and effective shooting range.

Ducks and geese are hunted mostly from waterside blinds, attracted into range with calls and decoys. Hunters may also sneak up on probable resting areas and shoot waterfowl as they are flushed. A variation of this jump-shooting is floating a river quietly, hoping to ease into range. Pass-shooting along routes where ducks and geese fly close to the ground is another tactic.

Adeptness at reloading is helpful for the blackpowder shooter hunting from a blind. He should be able to reload quickly to avoid missing chances for shots, yet safely because of the close proximity of other hunters. This is especially true of cramped or unstable boat blinds.

Waterfowl Hunting, an NRA Hunter Skills Series book, has the added information necessary to make your next waterfowl hunting trip a success.

Upland Birds

There is a complimentary relationship between blackpowder shotguns, good bird dogs, and close-flushing gamebirds in the uplands. Muzzleloading scatterguns are more than adequate for the job and add a certain charm to this exciting hunt.

Loads vary depending on the gun and type of bird you're hunting. The 20-gauge or even 28-gauge is fine for any upland birds, while a 12-gauge will offer a denser or bigger pattern, enhancing effectiveness or compensating somewhat for shooter error. The 12 is most versatile, handling light or heavy loads.

Recommended pellet sizes are No. 8 for quail, dove, and woodcock; 6 or 7 for grouse-size birds, and 5 or 6 for pheasant. Versatile double guns are best choked open in one barrel, modified in the other for most upland bird hunting.

Little in the way of tactics is involved in bird hunting. Locating good cover and dog handling are the most important areas. Experience and the power of observation will tell you how to locate the best cover for the bird you're hunting. Quail prefer dense creekbottoms or big fields with thick, high weeds. Doves are attracted to freshly cut cropfields where seeds have spilled on bare ground. Grouse like heavy, food-laden cover in woods, while woodcock prefer mature woods with an open, soggy floor. Sage grouse and prairie chickens like the open flats with their preferred foods, while chukars like grassy mountain meadows.

Photos by Mike Strandlund

Upland bird shooting with black powder and pointing dogs is an exciting way to hunt. Hunters walk the cover behind dogs until they get a point. Gunners flush the bird and shoot, and hopefully the dog returns with a bird for the bag. Patience comes into play as hunters wait for empty tubes to be reloaded so the hunt can resume.

Dog handling is a science unto itself. While some purists insist on classic pointer performance, good obedience and a desire to hunt are the most important attributes. Any dog that will stay close, work the cover, and not try to eat the bird you shoot will be an asset on a bird hunt. Pointers and retrievers are better in proportion to their training, and are a joy to watch in operation.

There are a few bird-hunting tactics that will help increase your bag. Early-season pheasants are typically easy marks, but learn fast. Later, hunters should hunt quietly to get into range. They should work cover in a way that traps roosters that have learned to run rather than fly.

Grouse, woodcock, and quail hunters—especially those without benefit of a dog—should work cover in a stop-and-go fashion. Birds will try to hold tight and let you walk past, but they can be worried into flushing if you stop and make them think they're spotted. As you hunt, stop in areas that provide good shooting lanes in the event you get a flush. Try to get birds to flush into crossing shots because on going-away shots, the smokescreen put up by the gun usually limits the muzzleloader hunter to one shot. Keep the sun out of your eyes. Mark birds that fall to prevent losses.

A chief limiting factor for the hunter pursuing birds with a muzzleloader is reloading time. Some shooting opportunities may be lost while you are rummaging in your bag for load components, measuring, and inserting them. To minimize this, keep your possibles well organized. Many hunters like to carry premeasured powder and pellet charges in 35mm film canisters. It can shave valuable seconds off your reloading time.

Rabbits and Squirrels

Both rabbits and squirrels may be hunted with shotgun or rifle, with a dog or without.

The classic squirrel gun is the .32-caliber rifle. Squirrels are preferably shot in the head, though riflemen usually must take whatever shot they can get on the hyperactive tree-dwellers. Shotguns with medium loads of 4 or 6 shot are better for limb-running squirrels.

Shotguns loaded similarly are the favorite arms of hunters after rabbits running through the briers or sagebrush. Sneak-and-peek hunters who try to catch rabbits or hares in their hides often use the smaller-caliber rifles, or perhaps a pistol.

Hunting dogs can aid hunters of small game. Beagles are a great help in flushing rabbits and hares from their thick cover.

Photos by Richard P. Smith

Rabbit and hare hunting can take many forms, from shotgunning winter-white snowshoes in the northern pines to plinking prairie jackrabbits with a rifle.

Photo by Mike Strandlund *Maslowski Photo*

Potting stew meat with a squirrel rifle has deep traditions in blackpowder shooting. Hunting these hyperactive tree-dwellers with patched ball and iron sights is an underrated test of marksmanhip and woodsmanship.

Squirrel hunters sometimes use dogs to locate squirrels and prompt them into moving into a position for a shot. Most squirrel hunters just find a place to hide among the trees, stay still, and wait for the squirrel that is sure to appear.

Predators and Varmints

Predator hunting, like blackpowder hunting, is a growing sport. It offers hunters a chance to hunt in the off-season to experience a new kind of hunting excitement, and in some cases to earn a little money on the side. Furbearers like coyotes, foxes, and bobcats may be called into shooting range with a call that sounds like a wounded rabbit. A blackpowder rifleman would do well with a .45 caliber and patience to make his one shot count. A shotgun with a heavy load of big pellets like BB is better in most cases for a surer shot and less pelt damage. Some hunters take predators, as well as varmints like woodchuck, by spotting them from a distance, stalking into shooting range, and making the shot.

Like predators, crows can be lured with a call. The call should simulate another crow, and a decoy of an owl—the crow's archenemy—also helps attract them. Since crows will decoy just into shotgun range in most cases, a potent load of No. 6 shot and a choked gun is recommended.

Photo by Stan Warren   *Photo by Russ Carpenter*

A good offseason sport is hunting varmints and predators with a muzzleloader. In some years, the valuable pelts of furbearers can help support the cost of your hobby.

CHAPTER 9

MUZZLELOADER HUNTING SAFETY AND ETHICS

Taking to the woods with a muzzleloader is a rich, rewarding sport that can give you a new perspective on shooting and hunting. But with this new perspective come new concerns for safety. Along with the usual safety procedures that must be adhered to while shooting or spending time in the outdoors, there are additional precautions necessary when using a muzzleloading firearm.

Four types of safety must be observed while hunting with a muzzleloader: general safety, muzzleloader/black powder safety, hunting safety, and general outdoor safety.

Gun Safety

The following safety rules apply to any type of situation in which a firearm is involved.

Photo by Mike Strandlund

1. Always have control of the gun's muzzle and keep it pointed in a safe direction.
2. Be positive of your target's identity before shooting.
3. Be prepared and take time to fire a safe shot. If unsure, or if you must rush so you cannot mount the gun correctly, pass up the shot. If there is any doubt whether you should shoot—don't.
4. Use the right ammunition for your firearm.
5. If you fall, control the muzzle. After a fall,

The key to safe gun handling is muzzle control. Be conscious of keeping the muzzle away from your body, especially when loading or cleaning.

185

check for dirt and damage and make sure the barrel is free of obstructions.

6. Unload or unprime your gun before attempting to climb a steep bank or traveling across hazardous terrain.

7. When you are alone and must cross a fence, unload or unprime your firearm and place it under the fence with the muzzle pointed away from your body. When hunting with others and you must cross a fence or similar obstacle, again place the gun in an unfirable condition. Have one of your companions hold the gun while you cross. Then take their unloaded or unprimed guns so your companions may cross safely.

8. Maintain your firearm, keep it clean, and never use a gun that is in poor condition, malfunctioning, or incapable of handling the ammunition you use.

9. Be aware of the range of your pellets or bullets. Buckshot and bullets can travel over a mile. Make certain that your pellets cannot rain down on other hunters, and remember that buckshot and bullets can ricochet off water, ground, and objects.

10. Adverse conditions and excitement can impair your mental and physical performance. Bulky clothing, rain, wind, and snow can cause poor gun handling and reduce your concentration on safety. Fatigue can cause carelessness and clumsiness, as can the excitement of a deer approaching. For maximum safety, control these conditions as much as possible.

11. Be conscious of your gun's safety or hammer, and remember to place it back in safe condition after the shooting opportunity has passed.

12. Establish zones of fire when hunting next to companions. Be sure your gun's muzzle is always pointing into your zone.

13. Alcohol, drugs, and hunting don't mix. Drugs and alcohol impair your judgment; keen judgment is essential to safe hunting.

14. When you have finished hunting, unload or disarm your gun immediately.

15. If companions violate a rule of safe gun handling, bring it to their attention and refuse to hunt with them unless they correct their behavior.

Photo by Mike Strandlund

Safe gun handling and caution in the field are the most important elements in muzzleloading hunting.

Photo by Mike Strandlund

Make use of muzzleloader safety equipment such as this frizzen guard, which acts as a safety to prevent the rifle from firing.

Muzzleloader Safety

The nature of muzzleloader shooting and handling leads to several possible safety hazards.

A chief potential for danger is in the carrying of quantities of gunpowder. Always be sure that the powder is kept in a closed container, and that when open it is not exposed to any form of heat or sparks. This means that you must never smoke or use any other kind of fire when a can of black powder or Pyrodex is open nearby. Never pour powder directly from the container into a gun's bore, where there could be a smoldering ember that might ignite the entire contents of the powder container. Keep all containers closed when you are shooting.

Be sure to use the correct gunpowder when shooting a muzzleloader. Use only black powder or Pyrodex of the correct granulation. Using a full charge of smokeless powder will almost certainly cause a muzzleloader's breech to explode.

When loading a muzzleloader, keep the muzzle pointed away from your face and body, and minimize the amount of time your hands are over the bore. Develop a loading system and concentrate on sticking to it—especially if you are using a double-barrel firearm.

Wipe out the bore of a muzzleloader after each shot. This will kill any spark that may remain in the breech, preventing an explosion when you recharge. It will also rid the bore of fouling, which impedes bore travel of the bullet and can be a safety hazard and inconvenience.

Prime a muzzleloader only after it is loaded and you are ready to hunt. Set the cap, prime the pan, and handle the lock very carefully, with the muzzle pointed in an absolutely safe direction, because this is the moment the gun has the best chance of discharging accidentally.

If the gun fails to fire when you attempt to shoot, keep the muzzle pointed in a safe direction for a few minutes. Do not remove the nipple or in any other way dismantle the gun. The misfire could be due to damp powder that is smoldering rather than burning, and which may ignite at any moment. Try again to discharge the gun by firing it. If the gun will not shoot, you will probably have to pull the load. Wait several minutes before attempting this. The safest approach is to soak the powder by pouring liquid down the barrel or through the flash hole before pulling the load. Be sure to clean and dry the gun thoroughly before reloading.

Hunt preparation time is a good time to review the manual

Photo by Rick Hacker

If a gun fails to fire, keep it pointed away from your body for several minutes to ensure a hangfire does not discharge in an unsafe direction.

that came with the firearm. If the manual has been lost or the firearm came without one, a note to the manufacturer will get a copy by return mail. Always stay within the manufacturer's recommendations!

If you have an opportunity to shoot an antique muzzleloader, have it checked thoroughly by a gunsmith first. Many antiques that appear to be in shooting condition are not. Whenever you borrow a muzzleloader or buy a used one, check carefully to make sure it is not loaded and it does not have functioning problems.

The smart hunter checks a firearm to make sure that parts and screws are tight and in good condition and that the lock operates properly. There are several hazards to look for in the lock area. Any looseness of fit that may have developed between the metal and wood parts of the lock and breech can cause poor ignition, which may lead to safety problems and poor accuracy. If tightening the screws and pins doesn't help, a blackpowder gunsmith should be consulted. The hammer should give no indication that it could slip from the half-cock position. Pulling the trigger should never result in a hammer-fall from half-cock. While you are checking the lock, make sure there is room inside the trigger guard to operate the trigger easily with your hunting gloves on, if you plan to shoot that way.

Many muzzleloading firearms of modern manufacture have double-set triggers for target shooting. With set triggers, the back trigger usually sets the front trigger on a lighter pull, which can aid accuracy in some cases. The rear trigger should not be used under field conditions. Concentration on the chase and higher levels of excitement while hunting make a light trigger pull a hazard in the field. You may safely use a set trigger for hunting by adjusting the pull of the front trigger to a heavier setting. Always recheck proper lock function after any adjustment of the trigger pull.

The action should be fit with safeguards to prevent it from firing accidentally. A leather frizzen boot is recommended on a flintlock to prevent the flint from coming in contact with the frizzen at an unplanned time. The caplock hunter should keep a piece of surgical tubing that will fit snugly on the end of the hammer, or a piece of soft rubber or leather to carry between the hammer and the nipple. This protects against unexpected ignition while providing a moisture barrier.

The ramrod used in the field should fit the thimbles of the firearm for ease of carrying. It must not extend in front of the muzzle enough to interfere with firing and it must be held tightly enough in the thimbles so it won't slip out when the gun is held muzzle-down.

Remember when using a wooden rod to use short strokes of four to six inches to seat the load. This method may prevent a nasty splinter wound from having a ramrod snap off under pressure.

Metal tips and ends may come off a ramrod during use and form a barrel obstruction if they are not fastened securely. This is easily prevented by pinning them into the ramrod. The pin is inserted through both the fitting and the ramrod. To keep the pin from pulling out of the end of a wooden rod, the pin should be installed across-grain.

Many people use a different ramrod for hunting than they use for target shooting. It is also quite common to use a different load for hunting from loads used for other shooting. Add to these two factors an increased likelihood that loading in the field is often amid distracting circumstances, and potential for errors rapidly increases. It is important, in checking the ramrod for hunting, to be sure it is plainly marked for its hunting load depth. This is done by setting the ramrod on a properly seated hunting load in the barrel of the muzzleloader. A mark is made around the ramrod where it touches the muzzle of the firearm. If the ramrod is scribed with a knife to mark it, the cut should be light so it doesn't weaken the rod.

While the muzzleloader is loaded, always carry the gun with the muzzle elevated to prevent a bullet or shot charge from slipping forward in the bore. In wet weather, use a balloon or piece of tape to keep rain or snow from entering the elevated muzzle and incapacitating the powder charge.

Some hunters who use primitive arms are tempted to wear the leather and fur clothing of the same era as their guns. Unfortunately, there are many more hunters today, many of whom have little hunting experience. Wearing clothes that may make you appear like an animal in areas where there are other hunters is strongly discouraged.

Safety in hunting areas can depend on having the equipment to deal with a mechanical problem. No hunting pouch is complete without a ball-puller, a patch-retriever, and a cleaning jag that fit the end of the ramrod being carried. Miscellaneous tools such as screwdrivers, files, and small locking pliers are also useful.

Also essential is a cleaning solution that will not freeze in a cold barrel and a patch lubricant that won't freeze or dry out under field conditions. A simple test for these qualities is to soak a patch in cleaner or lubricant and leave it overnight in the freezer section of a refrigerator. If it is dry or frozen in the morning, it's an unwise choice for cold weather hunting.

Some special precautions should be taken to prevent the hazards of barrel obstruction and wet powder during bad weather. All of the wood on a firearm and ramrod should be coated with a sealer to minimize its swelling and shrinking with moisture changes. When poor weather conditions are expected, a piece of black tape or a balloon can be placed over the muzzle of a rifle after it's loaded.

The flintlock action itself can be a source of injury to unwary bystanders unless the lock has been fitted with a flash guard. This metal sidewall for the pan is easily made and attached with the lock screw to redirect any spark and/or flash of flame upward when the gun is fired.

All of the gear required for muzzleloading and the ramrod extending from the front of the firearm create potential for snags. A hunter that protects the ramrod from getting caught in brush, fences, or the like is also protecting himself from sudden changes in muzzle direction. Cut down the chance of snags by wearing horns and bags high enough under the arm of the dominant hand so that they can be clamped firmly with the arm for activities such as running or bending. This also keeps them sheltered from brush.

Any time the firearm is carried across a barrier, up to a tree stand, or to a break for coffee, it should be in a safe condition. If it's a caplock, the cap should be removed and the hammer put down on leather or rubber. If it's a flintlock, the pan should be emptied, the frizzen opened, the flash hole plugged, and the hammer put down.

Before a gun is recapped or reprimed, it should be checked with the marked ramrod to determine that the ball or shot is still seated snugly on the powder charge. The percussion of firing one barrel of a double, the heat of the day, a jostle with the barrel pointed down, and any number of other circumstances can move a projectile away from the powder charge. As soon as this happens, it no longer has a load; it has a barrel obstruction.

A special situation exists when only one barrel of a muzzleloading shotgun is fired. While a modern shotgun is reloaded with the gun in much the same position as when it is fired, the muzzleloader is lowered and turned for reloading. As a result, the barrel that was on the shooter's right when fired becomes the barrel to the left when it is positioned for reloading. This could lead to double-charging one barrel, creating a safety hazard. Check with the ramrod whenever there's doubt.

Early in your experiments with shotgun loads, check to see if discharging one barrel of a double dislodges the load in the unfired barrel. If there is any chance it may, take steps to rectify the problem. Tighter wads are usually the key.

When reloading in the field, the powder supply should be replugged or covered as soon as the powder is measured. A hasty shot over an open powder horn can cause a grenade effect on the shooter's hip that would result in serious injury at best.

Eye protection while hunting is a must. Clear shooting glasses are fine and can also be used in all classes of target competition without conflicting with primitive equipment restrictions. Most people, however, prefer tinted or colored lenses. If you are going to invest in colored lenses, choose a tint that does not distort observed colors, especially hunter orange. Also, look for impact resistance. Most over-the-counter sunglasses will probably not do a good enough job for hunting situations.

NRA Staff Photo

Wearing eye protection while muzzleloader hunting is a good idea to prevent injury from a gun accident or tree branch.

Safety Afield

Many of the safety concerns a hunter must remember have nothing to do with guns. In fact, hunters are more likely to be hurt in an incident *not* involving a gun. They include the ever-present dangers of being in the woods: falls and similar mishaps, hypothermia, sickness, drowning, thirst, and starvation.

Being careful and not getting lost will prevent most of these. Use common sense; keep safety in mind. Always carry maps and a compass if there is a possibility of getting lost (even in familiar country) and know how to use them. Make sure that someone knows where you are going and when you plan to be back. Carry a first-aid kit, maybe a snake-bite kit, and signalling devices.

Photo by Mike Strandlund

Most dangers of being in the field can be averted by planning and using good common sense.

Hypothermia, or severe loss of body heat, is a little-understood affliction. It is one of the biggest threats to the outdoorsman, possible in temperatures as warm as 60 degrees under certain conditions. Wet clothes, wind, and fatigue contribute to hypothermia.

Persons suffering from hypothermia go through stages beginning with shivering and progressing to loss of muscular control, mental confusion, and unconsciousness. Victims may have very pale skin, rigid muscles, and may be unable to speak.

To help prevent hypothermia, wear clothes that offer good

protection in wind and wet, such as rainsuits or nylon shell jackets, combined with wool or good synthetic insulation. Dress in layers. Take precautions from getting wet. If you think there is a good chance of getting wet, you may be able to bring a change of dry clothes in a waterproof bag. Don't overexert yourself, as tiredness lowers resistance to cold. Carry sources of heat, such as warm drinks in thermos bottles, fire-building material, camp stoves, etc.

Hypothermia victims often don't realize the seriousness of the situation. They should be warmed with blankets, warm water, or the body heat of companions.

Photo by Mike Strandlund

Rugged terrain is a real danger to a hunter, especially if an injury from a fall could be complicated by cold weather or isolation from help.

Rugged terrain presents a variety of hazards to the hunter. There is the possibility of a fall. There is the chance that an older or out-of-shape hunter could become exhausted and have a heart attack. The danger of these situations is compounded because hunters are often far from help and by themselves.

In some areas, poisonous snakes, rabid animals, and other dangerous animals may pose a threat. Learn about these dangers, and take precautions.

Remember the best prevention for all problems afield are planning and common sense.

Hunting Safety

The combination of firearms, large numbers of hunters, limited visibility in woods, and other factors can create a dangerous situation. There are special hunting safety considerations:

- When hunting big game and upland birds, always wear an ample amount of blaze orange. Even if only a blaze orange hat is required, you should have more orange on the lower part of your body. When a hunter is shot by another because he is mistaken for a game animal, it is often because the shooter saw only the victim's dull-colored legs moving through brush.

Photo by Mike Strandlund

  Wear blaze orange pants or tie a piece of orange material around each leg. If you don't want to wear more than the minimum amount of blaze orange, supplement it with bright red clothing. This is almost as visible to another hunter, yet appears gray to colorblind game.

Always wear blaze orange whenever practical—especially where there are large numbers of hunters using rifles, and when required by law.

- Use a flashlight when moving through woods in darkness or twilight. This is the time when most accidents occur. If you have a flashlight, no one can mistake you for an animal. A light also helps prevent injuries from a fall or other accident.
- When field dressing or taking game from the woods, keep orange clothing visible. There is a tendency for hunters to remove their coats when doing these duties. They must be kept prominent, however, because this is the most dangerous time of the hunt.
- Use extreme care when hunting from tree stands. When getting into or out of your stand, momentarily clear your mind of hunting and everything else but safety. Always use a safety harness when entering, leaving, and occupying a tree stand. Deprime your gun and use a haul line to get it into and out of the stand—muzzle down, but making sure

the muzzle does not get plugged with dirt. Check the stand periodically to make sure it is in good condition, and be careful to install it securely. Some designs of portable tree stands are much safer than others. A tree stand hunter must also pay particular attention that he does not drop the gun from the tree, because the jar may cause the gun to discharge.

- Never shoot at sound or movement. Assume every sound you hear and movement you see is another hunter until proven otherwise. Never point your gun, cock the hammer, or put your finger on the trigger until you have positively identified the target as the game you want to shoot.
- Disregard peer pressure that places such urgent importance on being successful that it causes you to take chances.
- Be aware of "buck fever" and its prevention. Close encounters with game can cause the extreme excitement that causes accidents. Anyone is capable of unbelievable blunders at the sight of a trophy animal. Anticipation can make you see something that is not there. Chances of this are increased if the hunter is inexperienced, fatigued, or has poor eyesight. Ambitious hunters are tempted to take risks. But the right attitude, with safety foremost, greatly reduces the odds of a mishap.

Photo by Tom Fegely

All muzzleloaders, but flintlocks especially, are fire hazards when the woods are dry. After each shot in such conditions, check for a smoldering ember or patch that could start a wildfire.

197

- When hunting with companions, be certain of each other's location.
- If you're on land where you have sole permission to hunt, don't assume there are no other hunters around. That attitude may prompt you to take chances.
- Avoid areas with high hunting pressure.
- Remember that poachers and other irresponsible hunters may be nearby. Take every possible precaution—never assume that other hunters are safe.
- Use your knife safely, using special care not to cut yourself while field dressing an animal.

Hunting Ethics

Hunting ethics encompasses all the responsibilities a hunter has to other hunters, landowners, the general public, and the game. Governments require certain generally accepted ethical behavior

Photo by Betty Lou Fegely

An ethical hunter obeys all game laws. Most areas have a one-deer bag limit for muzzleloader hunters, and require them to tag their deer immediately upon recovery.

through hunting laws and regulations. But in most cases, it is up to the hunter to decide what is right and what is wrong, and to hunt according to those standards.

Some ethical questions in hunting are easy to answer. Others are tough. The standards of hunters cover a wide range. Most ethical questions can be resolved by answering these questions: Is it legal or, is it fair to everyone concerned, including the game, other people, and myself? There are laws and standards to follow, but ultimately, you must decide.

Responsibilities to Other Hunters

Besides safety, you have several other responsibilities to fellow hunters. If you find another hunter at the place you planned to make a stand, defer to him and find another site. It is counter-productive to challenge him to the spot. Hopefully, another hunter will someday show you the same respect.

Try to pass on responsible hunting behavior to fellow hunters. If a new hunter seems to be going astray, try to educate him in hunting ethics. If a companion refuses to hunt responsibly, refuse to hunt with him.

Don't litter, drive vehicles where others may be hunting, or otherwise disturb other people or the area. Most hunters have deep feelings for nature and the peace of mind they find while hunting. Don't violate them.

Responsibilities to Landowners

One example of how hunters hurt themselves through poor ethics is the alienation of landowners. Each year, thousands of acres of private land are posted off-limits because hunters treated the land or its owner with disrespect. It hurts all hunters.

Always get permission before hunting on any private property. Approach the landowner with courtesy—not only because you will have a better chance of getting permission, but because we all have a responsibility to promote the image of the hunter. Once you receive permission, treat the land with utmost care. Leave no signs you were there—take spent shells and litter with you, and maybe pick up some left by others. Don't drive on soft ground and leave tire ruts.

Other ways to keep good landowner relations are to avoid disturbing livestock, fences, crops, and other property. Don't abuse your welcome by bringing a carload of companions or hunting on the land day after day.

A token of appreciation such as a gift, a card, or offer to help with chores goes a long way toward being welcome next year.

Responsibilities to the Public

Remember that the environment and animals belong to everyone, not just hunters. Respect the rights of people who enjoy nature without hunting—avoid shooting in areas where you know nonhunters are enjoying the outdoors. Keep gut piles and other signs of hunting out of view. Don't display bagged animals to people who may not want to see them. Remember that unfavorable public opinion has resulted in laws and regulations that have hurt hunters.

Another duty the hunter owes the public is to ensure the enforcement of all laws. Hunters must abide by the laws and report those who trespass, poach animals, shoot road signs, or otherwise vandalize property.

Responsibilities to the Game

The game animal is more than a resource to be harvested. All game animals deserve the greatest respect a hunter can give his prey. Hunters who do not feel a deep reverence for wildlife and an obligation to conserve the resource are missing the essence of hunting.

Never take a shot that has a better chance of crippling than killing. Don't shoot beyond your accurate range and don't shoot at running animals that are near-impossible to hit. Don't shoot at an animal if another is standing directly behind it—the bullet could kill the first and wound the second. When hunting birds, always target a single bird—never shoot randomly into a flock or covey.

Responsibilities to Yourself

Don't forget your responsibilities to yourself. If a certain law or hunting regulation conflicts with your well-considered ethical beliefs, work to change that law. Fight it with letters and votes, not disobedience.

Don't take a chance or violate your ethics in a way you may regret later. At the same time, hunt hard, hunt honestly, and be proud of your sportsmanship.

Pass Along the Tradition

If you're a hunter in the truest sense, you will eventually reach a point where you derive the most hunting satisfaction from introducing others to the sport. It may be acquainting a friend with hunting, taking a young boy or girl on their first hunt, or volunteering in a hunter education program.

Talk with the new hunter about hunting responsibilities and ethics that all hunters should abide. Show respect for game by never taking a chancy shot, by making every effort to recover a wounded animal, and by never wasting bagged game. Make him or her realize why they must also treat landowners and the general public with respect, to prevent prejudice against hunters. Instruct new hunters early on safety, ethics and responsibility because their respect and appreciation of our hunting heritage will determine the future of hunting.

NRA Staff Photo

Perhaps our most important responsibility as sportsmen is to help others appreciate and respect our rich heritage as hunters. Sound knowledge and practice of hunting skills, safety, and ethics are needed for our sport to endure.

Appendix

Photo by Rex Thomas

THE NRA AND HUNTING

T he National Rifle Association encourages and supports sport hunting through a wide variety of programs and services.

The NRA Hunter Services Division assists state and provincial hunter education programs with support materials and training programs for professional and volunteer staff. NRA Hunter Clinics answer the demand for advanced education by emphasizing skills, responsibility, and safety as applied to hunting techniques and game species. The Hunter Information Service communicates to the members a variety of information necessary to plan and complete hunts. The NRA Youth Hunter Education Challenge offers a series of events on the local, state, and national levels to challenge young hunters, through hunting simulated events, to apply basic skills learned in the classroom. The NRA Hunter Recognition Program offers awards to hunters for all levels of hunting achievement. Financial support for wildlife management and shooting sports research is available through the NRA Grants-in-Aid Program.

The NRA Institute for Legislative Action protects the legal rights of hunters. NRA Publications provides a variety of printed material on firearms, equipment and techniques for hunters, including *American Hunter* magazine, the largest periodical in the U.S. devoted to hunting. Junior programs encourage young people to participate in hunting. Special insurance benefits are available to NRA hunting members, and hunters can further benefit by joining an NRA hunting club or by affiliating an existing club with the NRA. The NRA works with other hunting organizations to sustain a positive image of hunting as a traditional form of recreation, to combat anti-hunting efforts, and to promote a life-long interest in hunting.

For further information, contact the National Rifle Association of America, Hunter Services Division, 1600 Rhode Island Avenue, N.W., Washington, D.C. 20036-3268. Telephone (202) 828-6240.

NRA MATERIALS FOR THE MUZZLELOADER HUNTER

The following materials are available from the NRA Sales Department and can help you prepare for your next muzzleloader hunt.

DESCRIPTION	ITEM NO.	UNIT PRICE
The Hunter's Guide	HE5N5090	$8.95 each
NRA Hunter Skills Series		
Student Manuals		
Muzzleloader Hunting	HS5N5145	$5.00 each
Whitetail Deer Hunting	HS5N5047	$5.00 each
Western Big Game Hunting	HS5N5207	$5.00 each
Waterfowl Hunting	HS5N5083	$5.00 each
Wild Turkey Hunting	HS3N1043	$5.00 each
Hardbound Version		
Muzzleloader Hunting	HS5N5172	$14.95 each
NRA Basic Firearms Education Series		
Student Manuals		
The Muzzleloading Rifle Handbook	EZ5N1059	$2.00 each
The Muzzleloading Pistol Handbook	EZ5N2058	$2.00 each
The Muzzleloading Shotgun Handbook	EZ5N3057	$2.00 each
NRA Hunter Clinic		
Video Collection (VHS)		
Brochure/Order Form	HI3N5003	N/C
Successful Mule Deer Hunting	HS5N7107	$19.95
Rocky Mountain Elk Hunting	HS5N7170	$19.95
Black Bear Hunting Secrets	HS5N7303	$19.95
Successful Whitetail Deer Hunting	HS5N7063	$19.95
Life-Size Game Targets*		
Brochure/Order Form	HS3N0017	N/C
Package containing one each:		
Whitetail Deer, Turkey, Duck,		
Rabbit, Groundhog, Mule Deer,		
Black Bear, Pronghorn, Javelina,		
Coyote, Red Fox, Pheasant, and		
Squirrel	HS5N1023	$7.00

*Note: Various package quantities are available.

DESCRIPTION	ITEM NO.	UNIT PRICE
Other Brochures		
NRA Hunter Recognition Awards	HI3N0106	N/C
Wild Game From Field to Table	HI3N0080	N/C
The Hunter and Wildlife	HI3N0071	N/C
Landowner Relations	HE3N0033	N/C
Responsible Hunting	HE3N0024	N/C
Hypothermia	HE3N0079	N/C
Fitness and Nutrition	HE3N0097	N/C
Water Safety	HE3N0051	N/C
Tree Stand Safety	HE3N0015	N/C
Hunting's Future? It's Up To You	HE3N0159	N/C
Firearms Safety in the Field	HI3N0099	N/C
NRA and Hunting	HI3N0115	N/C
NRA Hunter Services Division		
Materials Price List	HI3N8091	N/C
NRA Standard Order Form	XS7N8000	N/C

ORDERING INFORMATION

* Use the NRA Standard Order Form to order items listed. Prices are subject to change without notice.

* Prices do not include shipping and handling charges. Certain state sales taxes are applicable.

* Order forms and current prices are available from NRA Sales Department, P.O. Box 96031, Washington, DC 20090-6031 or call **toll free 1-800-336-7402.** VA residents call **toll free 1-800-535-9982.** Hours: 9:00 a.m. to 5:00 p.m. Eastern time.

FUTURE NRA MATERIALS
FOR THE
MUZZLELOADER HUNTER

Other items for the muzzleloader hunter soon to be available from the NRA Sales Department:
NRA Hunter Skills Series
NRA Muzzleloader Hunter Clinic Instructor's Manual

NRA Hunter Clinic Camouflage Cap (Summer) and T-Shirt

NRA Hunter Clinic Blaze Orange Cap (Winter) and T-Shirt

THE NRA HUNTER SKILLS SERIES

T he NRA Hunter Skills Series is a developing library of books on hunting, shooting, and related activities. It supports the NRA Hunter Clinic Program, a national network of seminars conducted by the NRA Hunter Services Division and volunteer hunter clinic instructors.

The hunter training manuals are developed by NRA staff, with the assistance of noted hunting experts, hunter educators, experienced outdoor writers, and representatives of hunting/conservation organizations. The publications are available in student (bound) and instructor (loose leaf) editions.

The program is planned to include clinics and support material on hunting whitetail deer, waterfowl, wild turkey, small game, predators, upland game, western big game, and others. It will also address marksmanship and hunting with rifle, shotgun, muzzleloader, handgun, and archery equipment.

For more information about the NRA Hunter Clinic Program and its training materials, contact the National Rifle Association of America, Hunter Services Division, 1600 Rhode Island Avenue, N.W., Washington D.C. 20036-3268. Telephone (202) 828-6240.

NRA BIG GAME HUNTER AWARDS

L et the NRA Big Game Hunter Awards Program help preserve the excitement and memories of some of your best hunts. This program emphasizes the hunter's skills and quality of the hunt—not trophy size. Minimum requirements for all 14 categories of North American big game that are accepted for these awards are listed below. The program recognizes achievement in four different hunting methods:

Muzzleloading Firearm
Modern Firearm—Long Gun
Modern Firearm—Handgun
Bow and Arrow

Beautifully designed certificates mounted on walnut plaques are personalized with the hunt method, hunter's name, animal category and the year and the state or province of the hunt.

REQUIREMENTS

CATEGORY	INDEX FOR DETERMINING STATUS	MINIMUM REQUIREMENTS
Black Bear	Greatest width plus	16 inches
Cougar	length of skull	12 inches
Grizzly or Brown Bear	without jaw	18 inches
Elk	Minimum numbers	5
Mule Deer	of points	4
Black-tailed Deer	on at least	3
White-tailed Deer	one side	4
Coues White-tailed Deer	of rack	3
Moose	Greatest spread	40 inches
Caribou	Maximum inside spread	30 inches
Pronghorn	Length of	11 inches
Rocky Mountain Goat	longest horn	8 inches
Native Wild Sheep	Extent of curl	¾
Wild Turkey	Beard length	8 inches

For more information on the NRA Big Game Hunter Awards refer to the NRA Hunter Recognition Program brochure (HI3N0106) or contact the National Rifle Association of America, Hunter Services Division, 1600 Rhode Island Avenue, N.W., Washington D.C. 20036-3268. Telephone (202) 828-6240.

A Guide To
MUZZLELOADER HUNTING ACROSS NORTH AMERICA

Photo by Jim Hower

The following chart gives general dates for special big game hunting seasons with the muzzleloader only. Be sure to check with the state or provincial wildlife agency for specific season dates before you plan your hunt. Many agencies set seasons by management unit or zone, and these may change from one year to the next. Most states and Canadian provinces also allow muzzleloader hunting during their regular firearm season.

STATE/PROVINCE SPECIAL MUZZLELOADER SEASONS	MUZZLELOADING RESTRICTIONS
United States	
Alabama	
No special seasons	.40-caliber minimum
Alaska	
No special season	None
Arizona	
Deer-(mid-Oct-late Dec) Pronghorn-(late Sep) Elk-(late Sep-early Oct) Javelina-(late Feb-early Mar)	None
Arkansas	
Deer-(3 days mid-Oct)	.40-caliber minimum for deer
California	
Deer-(end Sep-early Dec)	Iron sights
Elk-Only (early Sep-early Dec) Antelope-(late Aug-early Sep) See zones	26-inch barrel, .40-caliber
Colorado	
Deer & Elk-(mid-late Sep)	.40-caliber minimum for big game or big game except elk & moose which have .50-caliber minimum
Connecticut	
Deer-State Land (3 days mid Nov)	.45-caliber minimum
Private Land (9 days mid Nov)	Round-ball only Round ball only
Delaware	
Deer-Special Statewide (mid Oct-3 days) or (3 days early Jan) Check regular shotgun season	.42-caliber minimum 28-inch barrel minimum 60-grain charge, no telescopic sights
Florida	
Deer-South Zone (3 days early Oct) Central Zone (3 days late Oct) Northwest Zone (3 days Nov)	.40-caliber minimum for deer; .20-gauge minimum (shotgun) for deer
Georgia	
No special seasons	.44-caliber minimum (rifle) for big game; .20-gauge minimum (shotgun); rifles legal for small game
Hawaii	
Legal during regular season. See regulations for certain local restrictions	.40-caliber minimum (rifle) Shotguns allowed for game birds

Idaho
Deer-(Nov-Dec) See units
Elk-(Nov-early Dec)
Antelope-(mid Oct)
Special permit during season
but legal during any controlled
big game hunts

.40-caliber minimum deer; .50-
caliber minimum elk; no telescopic
sights; black powder or pyrodex
only

Illinois
No special seasons

Singleshot muzzleloader only, rifle
permitted for deer hunting;.45-
caliber minimum; black powder or
pyrodex only

Indiana
Deer-(mid Nov)
Also during regular season
See regs

Singleshot muzzleloader only;
rifle permitted for deer hunting;
.44-caliber minimum (rifle) for
deer; handgun prohibited

Iowa
Deer-(9 days mid Oct) or
(mid Dec to early Jan)

.44-caliber minimum

Kansas
Deer-Early (9 days-mid Sep)
Regular (mid Dec-early Jan)

.40-caliber minimum; iron or peep
sights only during special season,
telescopic sights legal in regular
season

Kentucky
Deer-(second Sat in Dec)
See regs for closing date

.40-caliber minimum (rifle);
.20-gauge minimum (shotgun)

Louisiana
Deer-(7 days early Dec)
Legal for all game species in
season

.44-caliber minimum (rifle);
.10 gauge minimum (shotgun)

Maine
No special season

recommendations for deer: .440
round ball, 60-grain charge;
.50-caliber minimum for bear

Maryland
Whitetail & Sika Deer-(mid Dec-
early Jan); Can use in shotgun-
only areas for deer

.40-caliber minimum, 60 grains or
more black powder; no telescopic
sights

Massachusetts
Deer-Either sex (3 days mid Dec)

Primitive firearm license required;
18-inch minimum barrel; .44- to
.775-caliber

Michigan
Deer-Upper (9 days early Dec)
Lower (9 days mid Dec)

.44-caliber minimum

Minnesota
Deer-(10 days late Nov-early Dec)

none specified

Mississippi
    Separate primitive weapons license required for non-residents; No special season   .38-caliber minimum for deer; no telescopic sights

Missouri
    Deer-Special season (3 extra days after regular gun season) Special muzzleloader's license required   .40-caliber minimum; single shot; deer only

Montana
    Certain zones have season for archery, shotgun and muzzleloader only (early Sep)   No restrictions except for .45-caliber minimum in zones designated for archery, shotgun or muzzleloader only seasons

Nebraska
    Deer & Antelope-(3 days early Dec)   .40-caliber minimum

Nevada
    Deer-(15 days mid Sep)   Nonresident statewide quota of 105 bucks only

New Hampshire
    Deer-(10 days Oct-Nov)   .40-caliber minimum; Single shot only, rounds & maxi balls legal

New Jersey
    Deer-Bucks only (6 days early Dec); Either sex black powder by zone, (Dec 1-30 inclusive)   .44-caliber minimum; scopes not legal

New Mexico
    Deer-Special (mid Sep by zone) Turkey-Special; See regs   antlered deer only; 40-caliber minimum for deer

New York
    Deer-Bucks only (7 days mid Dec) Bear-By zones (7 days mid Oct)   44-inch barrel minimum; rifling in barrel, single projectile only

North Carolina
    Deer-(1 week); See regulations for dates   muzzleloading pistol not allowed

North Dakota
    Deer-(4 days Nov & 4 days Dec)   .45-caliber minimum deer
    Antelope-Reg season (mid Oct)   .44-caliber minimum antelope;

Ohio
    Deer-Special statewide (3 days early Jan); Bucks only in 3 areas (Oct)   12, 16, 20-gauge only (shotgun) .30-caliber minimum (rifle)

Oklahoma
    Deer-Bucks only (9 days late Oct)   .40-caliber minimum; no optical sights; muzzleloader pistols legal as second firearm only

Oregon
  Deer-By zone (Sep-Nov)
  Antelope-(Aug-Sep)

.40-caliber minimum deer, bear, antelope & cougar; .50-caliber minimum elk & sheep; iron sights only; open ignition allowed

Pennsylvania
  Deer-Flintlock only
  (10 days late Dec-early Jan)

.44-minimum caliber; flintlocks, roundball and open sights only; any gauge or type for shotgun

Rhode Island
  Deer-(mid Nov-early Dec)
  (12 days early Dec); See zones

.40-caliber minimum (rifle); .50 or larger smoothbore (20 gauge or larger); single projectile only

South Carolina
  Primitive firearms in certain
  Wildlife Management Areas
  (Sep-Nov)

.36-caliber minimum (rifle)

South Dakota
  Special seasons on 3 National
  Wildlife Refuges; Residents only
  (mid-Nov); See regs

.44-caliber minimum

Tennessee
  Deer-Muzzleloader only by unit
  (Oct-Dec); May be combined with
  archery in some areas; See regs

.40-caliber minimum; rifles, shotguns, handguns allowed

Texas
  No special seasons

No restrictions

Utah
  Elk-(9 days mid Sep)
  Mule deer-(9 days early Nov)
  See regs for units and season

.45-caliber minimum antelope; 40-caliber minimum deer; 50-caliber minimum other big game

Vermont
  Deer-(5 days late Nov-early Dec)

20-inch barrel minimum; .43-inch diameter minimum; single shot, single barrel

Virginia
  Deer-In certain western counties
  (Mid Dec-early Jan);
      Special bucks only season
  (6 days mid Nov); See regs

.45-caliber minimum deer; pistols legal for small game & nuisance wildlife

Washington
  Deer-Early (4 days Oct)
      Late (10 days Nov-Dec)
  Elk-Early (7 days early Oct)
      Late (Nov-Dec)

.40-caliber minimum; 20-inch barrel minimum

West Virginia
Deer-Special (5 days Dec)
Concurrent hunting permitted
using other arms

.44-caliber minimum; single shot,
iron sights only

Wisconsin
No separate season except special
hunt on Apostle Islands (month
of Oct)

.45-caliber minimum deer
(smoothbore); .45-caliber
minimum deer (rifle)

Wyoming
Antelope-Special (mid Aug)
Most blackpowder hunters
hunt during regular seasons

.40-caliber minimum; 50 grains
blackpowder minimum

Canada

Alberta
No special seasons

.44-caliber minimum

British Columbia
Special weapons hunts by
management unit; See regs

No restrictions

Manitoba
Registered guide required
for nonresident big game
hunters; No special season

No other firearms in possession;
.40-caliber minimum deer; .50-
caliber minimum other big game

New Brunswick
No special seasons

No caliber restrictions

Nova Scotia
No special seasons

.45-caliber minimum

Northwest Territories
No special seasons

Ammunition for bison and polar
bear must produce minimum of
2800 joules of energy at the muzzle

Prince Edward Island
No special seasons

No restrictions

Ontario
No special seasons

No restrictions

Quebec
No special seasons

No restrictions

Saskatchewan
Nonresidents need registered
guide for big game. Saskatchewan
Landing Provinical Park requires
primitive weapons only.

No restrictions

Yukon Territory
No special seasons

.45-caliber minimum for big game